Writing *to Be* Whole

A healing journal

EDDIE ENSLEY *and* ROBERT HERRMANN

LOYOLAPRESS.

CHICAGO

LOYOLAPRESS.

3441 N. ASHLAND AVENUE
CHICAGO, ILLINOIS, 60657

Cover design by Tracey Harris

Interior design by Eileen Wagner

ISBN 0-8294-1530-0

Printed in the United States

01 02 03 04 05 Brace 10 9 8 7 6 5 4 3 2 1

We dedicate this book to the people who helped, formed,
and inspired our ministry through the years:
Bishop J. Kevin Boland, who shepherded us with grace and humor
as our parish pastor and now as our bishop;
Bishop Raymond Lessard, who invited us to begin and guided us;
Fr. Tom Francis, O.C.S.O., whose joy and "holy foolishness" helped to launch us;
Sr. Mercedes Sullivan, who got in the trenches with us;
Fr. Tom Peyton and Fr. Bob Mattingly, who inspired us in our early days;
Fr. Richard Rohr, O.F.M., who believed in us and recommended us;
Georgia and Deacon George Foster, who have formed and loved us these last four years;
Mr. and Mrs. Irvin and Hedwig Herrmann, who have always been there for us;
and in memory of Fr. Ralph Tichenor, S.J., who modeled saintliness for us.

And also to a special friend and bright light from Eddie's childhood,
Sandra Carmack Underwood, who has become a bright light to both of us.

Table of Contents

How to Use This Book

This book is designed to be a pilgrimage, a journey of personal transformation. Through the time-tested practice of spiritual journaling, you will have the opportunity to look at your past and your present and take the whole of your life to a merciful God for healing. You can explore your spirituality, work on mending your relationships, and begin to see the world from a new perspective.

We have crafted journal suggestions to guide you as you journal. This book is designed so that you can write in it. You may want to use an extra notebook or sheets of paper as well so that you can further explore some exercises on your own. Your writing will come from your memories, your dreams, your prayers, and your meetings with God.

A SHORT HISTORY OF JOURNAL WRITING

Writing is one of the oldest and mightiest forms of self-discovery and prayer. Twenty-five hundred years ago, Jeremiah kept a journal of his anguish and his ecstasy in his prophetic encounter with God. Parts of his journal became holy Scripture. St. Augustine, in his *Confessions,* which is essentially a journal, told of his hurt, his shame, his rapture, and his visions. By putting his pen to paper, he dialogued with God, others, and himself. The more he wrote, the more he discovered. The more he discovered, the more his life changed.

As Augustine explored his soul through writing, he found his memories to be a pathway to God. One biographer summed it up this way: "Augustine sincerely experienced his memories as drenched in God's grace, which makes the memories testify, belatedly, to God" (Wills, xx).

Much of this journal will call you to remember, and in that experience of remembering, you will bump into the surprising presence of God and see your past in a different light.

Writing as a form of prayer does something no other form of prayer can do: it makes visible the invisible. We have lots of mental clutter, and underneath that clutter are the images, memories, stories, and thoughts that form our spiritual core. In writing, we get a chance to see the clutter, deal with it, and then draw out these treasures from our core. Writing makes this inner world concrete. Our problems become visible. And when we see them clearly, we can then hand them over to the God who comforts and mends.

Imitation of Christ, written by Thomas à Kempis, is, scholars believe, three different spiritual journals melded into one work. He used techniques that were popular at that time. One of those methods was dialoguing with Christ. The writer would pour out the feelings of his heart, connect with that part of himself that sensed God, and then write what he believed God's words to him would be. You will have the opportunity to use this technique in this journal.

In addition to his exploring in *Confessions*, Augustine explored hidden reality by dialoguing with different realities in a work called *Soliloquies*. For instance, he would set up a dialogue between himself and reason or truth. He would write a part for himself and a part for reason or truth, much like dialogue is written for a modern screenplay. He pioneered this technique and coined the word *soliloquy*, which means "a dialogue with oneself." Many spiritual journalists followed his lead, dialoguing not only with abstract concepts but also with God, the Virgin Mary, or other sacred personages. The medieval miracle and mystery plays performed in churches brought this type of dialogue with God and with spiritual realities such as truth or reason to the common people. The dialogues in this book are inspired by this long history.

In another work, Augustine set up imaginary dialogues with real human beings—priests, friends, and others. He imagined what they might say and put words in their mouths that were based on their perspectives. His book of imagined dialogues with friends who helped him explore spiritual reality is called *Happiness in This Life* (Wills, 50–51). Early journal keepers, such as Thomas à Kempis, also worked with guided meditations, in which the writer imagined Christ in a situation and talked with him. You will have a chance to use this technique of spiritual discovery throughout this journal.

HOW THIS TYPE OF JOURNALING CAN HELP YOU

Evangelical theologian Richard Peace writes in his book *Spiritual Journaling,* "For most of us, life is like an MTV video: all sorts of things are happening, flung at us rapidly in small doses. What does it all mean? Who are we in the midst of all this input? Journals help us make sense of what's happening to us" (Peace, 23).

We have designed this book to exercise your sacred sensors, your visionary side. Scientists and theologians are now saying that we are actually designed to experience God. Living in a busy, hectic world that often discounts spiritual experiences allows the visionary part of us to atrophy. Our spiritual lung capacity shrinks; our spiritual heartbeat grows weak. Writing helps the visionary part of us come to life again.

Not only is journaling good for our souls, it's also good for our bodies. Dr. James Pennebaker, research psychologist at the University of Texas at Austin, has gathered a number of impressive studies on the effect of journal-style writing on both mental and physical health.

He divided students into two groups. One group was asked to write daily on emotionally and spiritually charged topics. Another group of the same size was asked to write daily on superficial topics. The students who explored their inner life ended up having 50 percent fewer visits to the student health center than the students who wrote only on superficial topics. Laboratory tests showed wide differences in the immune systems of the groups. The lab results of the test on the group that journaled thoughtfully showed a measurable immune-system boost that remained strong long after the study.

The pilgrimage you will take with this book will help you deal with the here and now. It will place in your hands the same tools that Jeremiah, Augustine, Teresa of Ávila, Hildegard of Bingen, and many of the great rabbis used, tools for praying on paper. You can test solutions for daily problems and write in ways that lessen stress. You will learn to sum up the day on paper and give it to God in prayer.

You may be asking yourself, "Is this just one more thing I can fail at?" For many people, the idea of writing carries with it some inhibiting baggage from the past. Perhaps you remember papers returned with red marks all over them. You might think of how many good projects you started and then failed to complete. Maybe you worry that your writing won't equal Teresa's, Augustine's, or Jeremiah's. Well, I have some powerful reassurance for you. What you are writing is for yourself. It's between you and God. No teacher will correct it. Don't worry about spelling, grammar, or neatness. Don't worry about writing profound prose.

We knew a man who said that he tried to pray every day, but failed. He was frustrated because he just couldn't get it right. We said to him, "Trying to pray *is* praying." Suppose your six-year-old came home from school with a picture of purple grass, a green sun, and a smudge for a house. Scrawled at the bottom in misspelled words is the message "Momy I luve you." Would you say that your child failed at loving you? Trying to love God *is* loving God. There is no such thing as trying to write a spiritual journal and failing.

All you need to do to succeed in the journal/prayer exercises in this book is put pen or pencil to paper and make a mark. It doesn't matter what comes out. It matters that you begin, that you try. That act starts the flow, and the flow is what is important.

Many people find that making an initial commitment and finding a special time every day to journal provides the discipline they need to stay with the journey. If making this kind of commitment to other disciplines has helped you in the past, then of course let it work for you now.

Perhaps you have tried to make a daily commitment to prayer or journaling before and it just didn't work for you. Don't set yourself up to start something and stumble again. Journal when you feel the urge. Begin and you will soon find that you can't stop. Write your way through this book at your own pace.

There is always value in starting at the beginning and going through to the end. Each section of this book, to some extent, builds on the sections that came before. But you might prefer to skip around, thumbing through the pages until you find a section that entices you.

You might get absorbed in the exercises and finish this book in a week. Or you might take months, going through it a bit at a time. This is your journey; go at your own pace in your own way and in God's time.

A WORD ABOUT THE EXERCISES IN THIS BOOK

A journal differs greatly from a diary. A diary is a record of daily events; a journal is a tool for uncovering the textures of your soul. You explore memories, feelings, and visions. You test out problems in relationships. You pray, you meditate, you anguish, you laugh—all on paper.

Most of us weren't taught how to do all of this. The purpose of this book is to systematically introduce you to journaling techniques that have been proven over time.

Using springboards is one of those techniques. Springboards are phrases that draw you into writing. Drawn from the themes of the old masters of spiritual journaling, the springboards we have provided don't so much teach you to write as entice you to write.

The second method we use combines springboards and an ancient prayer practice of the church: the guided meditation. Imaginative meditations aid self-exploration and inner healing. In times past, meditations that pictured sacred scenes, usually from Scripture, were frequently used to awaken the visionary side of people's souls. Great leaders such as St. Anselm, St. Bonaventure, and St. Ambrose wrote such meditations. People packed into churches whenever priests or friars read these meditations, and powerful healing occurred.

Wandering Franciscan friars taught illiterate people to make up holy narratives based on Bible stories they remembered and to put their pain and joy into the narratives. This book uses this method, except you get the chance to enter into the scenes with your writing.

This book includes guided meditations to stimulate your prayerful self-exploration. A good way to begin is to read over the meditation one or two times, then close your eyes and carry yourself through it, answering in your head the questions we've provided. Then, after going through the meditation mentally, begin writing. The answers that come to you when you start writing may be different from the ones that came to you when you went through the meditation in your head. Fresh inspirations may surprise you as you write. You may find that as soon as you read the prompts, you want to begin writing without first going through the meditation mentally. If that works for you, then by all means begin writing as soon as you feel the inspiration.

Also, don't worry about how vividly you imagine the scenes. Your imagination does not have to be in Technicolor; just having a sense of the scene is enough.

Avoid the temptation to go through the meditations only in your mind. You will receive benefit if you do, but you will miss out on the mighty transformation that comes from actually setting pen or pencil to paper. Even if you write only a sentence or two when there is room to write a page, that act will make visible what is hidden in your soul.

—Eddie and Robert

I *Finding Your Here and Now*

You are embarking on a writing journey. You will pass through many landscapes. You will experience the spiritual equivalents of mountain trails, raging waters, peaceful valleys, and frightening heights. You will gaze through the fog and the distance into the past. You will look at relationships, at the people who are your companions through life. You will look at the horizon, that mysterious part of every landscape that points into the unseen homelands of God.

The first landscape is the present moment. Where are you now? The aim of this chapter is to anchor you in your present. Take a close look at the ground you walk on every day. It's important to see exactly where your feet are before you begin any journey.

In a moment you will have a chance to anchor yourself in the present moment, which God can make fresh and new.

In this chapter, you will

- describe your tensions and joys
- discover letter writing as a means of prayer

PRAYER OF ENTRANCE

Dear God,
I begin the first steps of my journey.
I write the first words of this healing journal.
Guide my thoughts and my hand.
Help me see more clearly the contours of my soul,
the patterns of my thoughts.
Help me touch this moment, this present,
and give it to you, that you may flood me with your love
and show me the seeds of eternity
hidden in the ordinary things.
Amen

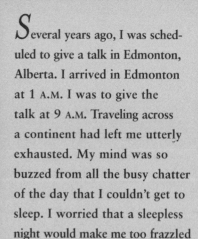

Several years ago, I was scheduled to give a talk in Edmonton, Alberta. I arrived in Edmonton at 1 A.M. I was to give the talk at 9 A.M. Traveling across a continent had left me utterly exhausted. My mind was so buzzed from all the busy chatter of the day that I couldn't get to sleep. I worried that a sleepless night would make me too frazzled to give a good presentation.

Instead of tossing in bed, I decided to pull out my journal. I began writing about what was happening right then. "My joints ache, my thoughts scatter everywhere, I'll probably stumble through every talk tomorrow." I kept writing out my little distresses and anxieties of the moment. I even wrote out my anger about the slow customs line at the airport. Soon, calm replaced panic. As I named and described my aches and tensions, they lessened or disappeared. I felt God in the midst of my tiredness. I fell into a restful sleep.

(Continued)

The talk I gave the next morning was not only one of the most powerful I have ever given, but it was also marked by peacefulness. My journaling had emptied me of the frustrations of the moment. By anchoring me in the now, my writing made space in my heart for God.

—Robert

GETTING STARTED
Complete these sentences.

A word that describes my life right now is

If I drew a picture of my life right now, I would draw

Some things that have made me happy lately are

Some things that have bothered me lately are

Some actions I've taken lately that I feel good about are

Some actions I've taken lately that I regret are

A GUIDED MEDITATION: YOU MEET JESUS

Throughout this journal, you will use a powerful tool for transformation, the guided meditation. Guided meditations employ the imagination to vividly carry you into sacred scenes. The Scriptures and the Christian and Jewish traditions abound with these meditations. The Twenty-third Psalm is the most celebrated scriptural guided meditation. The psalmist's words transport readers into a sacred meadow and place them beside still water. Ignatius of Loyola, the founder of the Jesuits, popularized imaginative meditations that brought readers into Gospel scenes. The guided meditations in this book build on this rich history.

In preparing for a guided meditation, do whatever makes you comfortable. This can include putting on soft music, sitting in a favorite chair, and closing your eyes.

Get comfortable and ready to imagine . . .

Jesus enters the room. He stands behind you and places his hands on your shoulders. His touch is firm and reassuring. A light surrounds him, and you feel it surround you too. This light makes you calm and warm.

What passes through your mind as you become aware of the light from Jesus surrounding you?

_____

_____

_____

You sense an eternal love entering your life through Jesus' hands. It fills your body as well as your soul. You sense your tensions passing into Jesus' hands. What are some of those tensions?

_____

_____

_____

Jesus speaks to you. "It's human to have tensions. When you acknowledge and name them, they lose much of their power. And as you name them, you can turn them over to holy love. When you name your tensions and write them out, they begin to fade. Then you can become aware of more important and fundamental aspects of your life. You can pay attention to more central realities, such as joy.

"What has been the great joy of your life lately, the happy reality that has most engaged you?"

_____

_____

_____

When you finish writing about the joy, you notice that Jesus is no longer standing behind you, but has moved more fully into your heart.

Now that you have explored your tensions and joys with Jesus, you can better see the ways in which your life needs healing. Write Jesus a letter explaining this.

Dear Jesus,
These are the ways I need healing in my life right now:

_____

_____

_____

_____

_____

_____

_____

If Jesus were to write you a letter telling you how to discover healing in your life, what would he write?

_____

_____

_____

_____

_____

_____

_____

MEDITATION FOR CLOSING

Meditate on Psalm 118:24:

> This is the day that the LORD has made;
> let us rejoice and be glad in it.

Take a few moments to write a response to this verse.

_____

_____

_____

_____

_____

_____

2 *Meeting the God Who Comforts*

In the last chapter, you had a chance to anchor yourself in the present. This kind of anchor is important if you are to go exploring. This is a critical journey. If you want healing for your soul, eventually you will have to look at your deepest fears, express your most keenly felt regrets, and describe your losses. But this healing journey is not along a lonely pathway or through a solitary valley. The landscape may become rough, but walking beside you along the way will be the one who dries your tears and warms your heart with a comfort that flows from eternity.

You need to feel safe when you explore the landscape of your soul. When you feel safe, you can stare down your fears and see yourself honestly. You can even look beyond ordinary sight and read what's really on your mind.

You will find safety when you meet the God of all comfort. And, oddly enough, you can meet God in your own memories. Even people who have much pain in their lives can uncover memories of good experiences. These are the memories that need tending. You can cultivate the good moments in your life, even moments from long ago. And when you discover those memories, you will find within them God's presence.

Your memories of love and of God's presence can be moments of healing and celebration. When you find these jewels from the past and celebrate them, you will be better able to step forthrightly into the life that God intends for you in the present.

You cannot manufacture God's comfort, for it is free. It is a gift. But while you cannot generate comfort, you can ask for it, you can say yes to it, and you can make space in your heart for it.

Jesus Christ spoke of this safety, this peace that abides in the mystery of the brightness of God, when he said, "Peace I leave with you; my peace I give to you. I do not give to you as the world gives" (John 14:27).

Early in my spiritual journey I discovered the power of memory to put me in touch with comfort.

About twenty years ago, soon after I began journaling, I was weighed down with anxiety. It was my freshman year at Columbus State University, and it seemed certain that despite my studying five hours a day, two of my three grades would be Cs. My anxiety had become so strong that I couldn't even concentrate on my studies. I hadn't been journaling very long, but that day I scrawled, "I need comfort and assurance."

From a place deep inside me I heard a reply: "I will teach you about comfort."

Right then a memory from my early childhood emerged, and I started writing about it. Just putting my pencil to paper strengthened the memory. The words I wrote transported me back to my grandparents' house in Texas.

(Continued)

Here's what I wrote:

I awoke in an unfamiliar bedroom to the smell of bacon and eggs frying. Everything was bright with sunlight. As I stretched lazily in bed, conversations filtered in from the kitchen. I heard my grandfather's strong, distinct voice roll through the hallway as he drank coffee with my father. Hearing the grown-ups talk made me feel happy and safe.

When I finally shook the sleep off and padded my way into the kitchen, everyone turned and looked at me. I couldn't help but grin at those welcoming faces. It felt like sunshine to hear their greetings as I approached.

As I wrote about that safe and happy time, the memory chased away many of my present anxieties. My head was cleared for studying, and I ended the semester with good grades after all.

—Robert

In this chapter, you will

- remember and write about past times of comfort

- meet Jesus in a guided meditation and hand your fears over to him

PRAYER OF ENTRANCE

Dear God,
I ask your Spirit to guide
my thoughts as I remember
and my hand as I write.
Gently lead me into your ease,
so that I can extend your peace to all I meet
and become for others a sign of your peace.
Surround me with your great peacefulness,
calm my heart, and make me ready
to meet you in my writing
and in my prayer.
Amen

ENTER A SAFE PLACE

You have within you the memories of all the times you were comforted and made to feel safe. When you connect with those times, the comfort will return.

Recall a time from your early childhood when you felt that the world was safe and bright. Tell the story here.

_____

_____

_____

_____

_____

_____

_____

_____

If I were to draw a picture that depicted safety, I would draw a picture of

_____

The person who most helps me feel safe is _____

The last time I felt God's comfort was when

_____

The scene from the Bible that brings me the most comfort is

_____

The Bible passage that most comforts me is

_____

The music that most comforts me is

_____

What did completing these sentences reveal to you about yourself?

_____

_____

_____

_____

_____

_____

_____

DISCOVER A LETTER FROM GOD

God is ready to comfort you. God's voice resounds throughout creation. God also speaks through sacred Scripture. God whispers to your soul, speaking in what Elijah calls "the still small voice." You can listen to God by searching your heart. You can externalize that voice through writing. Because you are human, you hear imperfectly, incompletely. Yet you do hear.

This exercise is simple. If God wrote you a letter to comfort you, what would that letter say? Set your pen to paper and begin writing.

A GUIDED MEDITATION: JESUS COMFORTS YOU

Get comfortable and ready to imagine . . .

Someone comes into the room to join you. It is Jesus. He has come to hear about your anxiety and to offer you comfort. He sits facing you. His eyes carry no condemnation, only concern.

Rest in his gaze for a moment. Here's a friend who wants to support you. Allow Jesus' presence to comfort you.

As your eyes meet Jesus' eyes, what do you feel?

_____

_____

Both of you are surrounded by light. It makes you feel at home. Describe this light and the effect it has on you.

_____

_____

Now, Jesus speaks. His words make you feel comforted and safe. This is what he says:

_____

_____

After you have listened to Jesus, you reply:

_____

_____

Jesus now asks you to extend your arms, hands out and palms up. He places his hands on yours. Your fears and tensions leave you and enter Jesus. Many of these fears and tensions are deep-seated; maybe you haven't even named them yet.

You actually see tension cross Jesus' face as he absorbs your anxieties.

Jesus says, "I love you. I am always here to calm and comfort you. I want you to tell me your fears. It is safe for you to name them. Just write them out for me."

Write down as many fears that come to you. (You may need additional pages.) After you write down each fear, write what you think Jesus' response would be.

I am afraid of

_____

Jesus comforts me, saying:

_____

_____

_____

I am afraid of

_____

Jesus comforts me, saying:

_____

_____

_____

I am afraid of

_____

Jesus comforts me, saying:

_____

_____

_____

I am afraid of

_____

Jesus comforts me, saying:

_____

_____

_____

I am afraid of

_____

Jesus comforts me, saying:

_____

_____

_____

MEDITATION FOR CLOSING

Meditate on Matthew 11:28–30:

> *Come to me, all you that are weary and are carrying heavy burdens, and I will give you rest. Take my yoke upon you, and learn from me; for I am gentle and humble in heart, and you will find rest for your souls. For my yoke is easy, and my burden is light.*

Take a few moments to write your response to this passage.

_____

_____

_____

_____

_____

_____

_____

3 *Facing Your Fears*

In the last chapter, you met the God of comfort. As you taste this deep-down peacefulness, you will often find that you are free to face some of your most entrenched fears. In the last chapter, you took some of your easy-to-find fears to God, the fears that came to your mind right away. In doing this, you opened yourself to God's ease and peace.

In this chapter, you will face the harder fears, the fears of which you are not always conscious. You will meet a God who will gently help you face those hidden fears in a way that is right for you.

Sometimes the fears that cause the most stress lie so deep inside you that you can't contact them by simply trying to think about them. These are the fears that you push beneath the surface in order to hide them away and forget them. Patrice O'Connor, registered nurse, health expert, and author, says, "Stress is like an iceberg. We can see one-eighth of it above, but what about what's below?" Only when peace comes to you will these fears emerge. They will surface at their own pace, on their own schedule. There is no need to strain and search for them. They will emerge when you feel safe.

In this chapter, you will

- face your fear through a guided meditation

- name your fear

- write stories of the times when you have been comforted

A friend of mine, a Presbyterian minister, finally retired at age seventy-five after forty-eight years in the ministry. The last twenty-five of those years he spent as pastor of a thousand-member parish, putting in fifteen-hour workdays right up to the time of his retirement.

Suddenly he found himself with lots of time on his hands. Yes, retiring was the right thing to do. But a gathering unease nagged him. At times, especially when he was reading a novel or watching the history channel—both totally new pleasures to him—his heart would start rocking like a boat in a swell. And for just a moment, a sense of horror and failure would clutch at him.

His pastorate had been a success. His children had turned out fine. He and his wife had a stable and comfortable retirement. Why the dread?

The answer came one night in a dream. He dreamed he awoke in

(Continued)

the night and began looking desperately for something, though he didn't know what it was. He opened the closet door and began rummaging through a stack of old clippings. Then he saw his picture on one of the clippings; it was his obituary.

He awoke from the dream trembling. He woke up his wife and recounted his dream. She held him and prayed with him.

Later he visited a close minister friend, who prayed with him, read him comforting Scripture, and listened to him. Like the hundreds he had comforted, my friend knew he now needed comforting.

For years he had ministered to others who feared death. He'd cared for them in hospitals and served at their funerals. He thought he had faced down the dread of death long ago. Yet now, when he was still healthy and vital, he faced a dread so strong and deep that it seemed primal.

(Continued)

PRAYER OF ENTRANCE

Dear God,
I guide my prayer and my writing
as I face my buried fears.
I hand fear over to the comfort and love
that surround my every breath,
the mystery that follows my every step.
This mystery abides with me
in times of desolation,
accompanies me when I'm in despair,
revives me in my seasons of consolation,
and banishes the dark and the shadows.
I hand over my tension, my fears, my anxiety.
Soften my heart with your nearness.
Shine your light along the roads I take.
And always, in every place, may I soothe,
comfort, and cherish others
in the way that you soothe, comfort, and cherish me.
As I face my fears,
help me become an emblem of your healing,
a quiet presence along the way,
one who comforts others with your presence.
Amen

The last time I felt free to pour out my fears to someone was when

___

The last time I poured out my fears to God was when

___

If I wanted to help someone feel safe, I would

___

What are some of the images that comfort and quiet your soul? Write them down.

_____

_____

_____

What do you do to nurture yourself, to renew your spirit?

_____

_____

_____

Throughout Christian and Jewish history, many visions were reported to have occurred in dreams. Such graced dreams helped people face their fears and experience God's consolation.

It is time for you to have a vision in a dream. In this dream you will face a great fear and accept a great comfort.

Enter this dream vision only if you feel safe and ready to face a fear that you might have been pushing below the surface.

A GUIDED MEDITATION: YOU FACE YOUR FEAR

Get comfortable and ready to imagine . . .

Jesus comes up behind you and places his hands on your shoulders. You feel the anxiety leave you. The warmth comes. You notice a subdued light emanating from Jesus.

You feel safe enough, relaxed enough, to float. You dream.

You find yourself in a wooded field in the middle of the night. Stars glisten all across the sky above you. You've felt this awe before. You have known the comfort of the glittering night sky. In the past it has spoken to you of the incomprehensible, but in a way that made you feel calm.

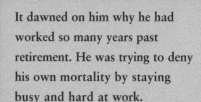

It dawned on him why he had worked so many years past retirement. He was trying to deny his own mortality by staying busy and hard at work.

For a few months, my friend let others minister to him for a change. They helped him face his fears. Finally he was able to enter a place of inner rest.

—Robert

You sit in the grass and stare up at this sacred canopy. You remember other times you have experienced this silent ease.

Write about some of the times you have looked out at the night sky and tasted God's eternity—and God's calm.

_____

_____

_____

_____

_____

_____

_____

Now an angel stands behind you, lighting up everything around you. At first you are afraid, but it is an awe-filled fear. Along with the fear, you feel God's reassurance. You know that this angel, sent by God, has come to accompany you as you face your fears.

In the presence of this light I feel

_____

Now the angel steps in front of you, and you see the angel clearly. Describe this angel.

_____

_____

You now speak to the angel. This is what you say:

_____

_____

_____

The angel replies, and what the angel says comforts you. This is what the angel says:

_____

_____

_____

Now the angel asks, "Are you ready to face a hidden fear?"

You reply: _____

The angel leads you toward a hill. In the bright starlight you can barely make out the entrance to a cave. The cave holds the fears you have postponed facing. The angel slowly guides you toward the cave.

You somehow know that what you will see inside the cave's entrance will symbolize one of your fears. For the retired minister in the story at the beginning of this chapter, the symbol was his obituary. For another person, it was an old report card with lots of Cs, Ds, and Fs, symbolizing her fear of failure.

You approach the cave, but you are not close enough to peer inside. You do not know what symbol you will see in the cave's entrance. The angel goes before you, lighting the way.

The angel then lights up the entrance, and you see a symbol of a hidden fear. Look at the symbol for a moment.

Describe what you see.

_____

_____

_____

Describe how this symbol makes you feel.

_____

_____

_____

Now it is time to name the fear. What do you name it? _____

Big fears that lie beneath the surface affect your daily living. They sap your energy. They grip you at inopportune moments.

How does this fear affect your daily living?

_____

_____

_____

_____

_____

_____

_____

_____

_____

The angel speaks to you: "Your fear did not come in an instant nor will it leave in an instant. The first step in living free of your fear is to acknowledge it. You have begun that process. Your next step is to give your fear to God. Each time the fear emerges, acknowledge it and hand it over to the sacred mystery that surrounds you and your world."

The angel continues: "The comfort of God comes to us through more than our praying and our meditation. The comfort of God comes to us through others."

The angel pulls out a scroll and says: "Write some stories of times others have comforted you when you were afraid."

Write one or more stories here.

_____

_____

_____

_____

_____

_____

_____

_____

_____

_____

The angel says: "Memory is a mighty form of prayer. Memory summons the presence that brought the consolation, the insight or healing."

Now write one or more stories of times when God comforted you.

_____

_____

_____

_____

_____

_____

_____

_____

_____

_____

_____

_____

_____

_____

_____

_____

_____

MEDITATION FOR CLOSING

Meditate on Isaiah 40:1–5:

> Comfort, O comfort my people,
>   says your God.
> Speak tenderly to Jerusalem,
>   and cry to her
> that she has served her term,
>   that her penalty is paid,
> that she has received from the LORD's hand
>   double for all her sins.
> A voice cries out:
> "In the wilderness prepare the way of the LORD,
>   make straight in the desert a highway for our God.
> Every valley shall be lifted up,
>   and every mountain and hill be made low;
> the uneven ground shall become level,
>   and the rough places a plain.
> Then the glory of the LORD shall be revealed,
>   and all people shall see it together,
>   for the mouth of the LORD has spoken."

Take a few moments to write your response to this passage.

_____

_____

_____

_____

_____

_____

4 *Recovering from Your Past*

In the last chapter, you had an opportunity to face some fears from your past. Now you will look at the bigger picture of your past. Your life has both joyful and sorrowful mysteries (if you're Catholic, think of the joyful and sorrowful mysteries of the rosary). These mysteries are intertwined. They help form the whole of your life.

"Try an expedition into your past to discover how it influences your present," says journaling therapist Kathleen Adams, who directs the Center for Journal Therapy in Lakewood, Colorado. This chapter will help you recover forgotten memories and images. Once you have done so, your reminiscences will flow freely, transforming you.

You remember much more than you realize. But you often pay little heed to those memories. They are more like bubbles that come to the surface, burst, and then disappear without accomplishing anything. If you want healing for your soul, you must give memory proper regard. You must name the symbols and images that your memory churns up. Then you can write them down and tap their full potential to give grace to your life.

This is the time in your journaling to recount the blessed times and let the melodies and rhythms of those times work their healing resonance in your soul. As the mystery of joy unfolds, you will feel safe enough for the sorrow to edge its way toward the surface.

As you remember, you will discover and tell the stories of your life. More and more healers—clerics, psychotherapists, physicians, and those who teach spirituality—are emphasizing the role of storytelling in healing.

In this chapter, you will

- make various lists to guide your remembering

- use those lists to explore your life story

- explore your past with mapping exercises

I have kept a journal since I was sixteen. That may seem too young to start a spiritual journal, but an unexpected spiritual event turned my life around and started me on a spiritual pilgrimage. I had a teenage brush with the law. I was caught in the presence of a friend who was shoplifting. The only real punishment was seeing the profound disappointment in my parents' eyes when they picked me up at the police station. That evening, in my shame and confusion, I was met by the unexpected grace of God. As I lay in bed, weeping over the day's events, my tears began to change, and the heavy weight that was bearing down on me began to lift. Something I could not explain or control began to wash my spirit and mind. While I heard no voice and saw no lights flashing from the sky, an unmistakable presence of love enveloped me, a love that seeped into every aching cell of my body. God began to touch every shadow of despair inhabiting my mind;

(Continued)

his love began to fill me with an inner warmth and brilliance. I didn't understand how I could feel hopeful at this point, but what was happening inside of me was out of my hands. Hope and courage put me to sleep that night, and as I reflect on that night now, I believe I knew that my life had just turned a corner. What that meant has taken years to unfold.

I began to attend church regularly. I had a deep desire for long periods of quiet contemplative prayer, though I didn't know the word *contemplative* at the time. I wanted to rest in quietness in the presence of the one who had touched my heart and turned my life around.

I began to reprioritize my days so that I could have time for prayer, sometimes an hour or more every day. A riot of powerful holy sensations streamed through me, without order. I had no one to listen to what was happening inside me. My

(Continued)

PRAYER OF ENTRANCE

Merciful and loving God,
I begin to look at the story of my life,
to discover its plot, its themes.
Help me celebrate the joy
and honestly face the sorrow.
Open my eyes so that I can see
your footsteps and interventions
throughout my life's journey.
Help me see my story
as a story of redemption.
Enfold me in your tenderness
as I look at the pain.
May the healing that comes to me
bring me new strength to love and serve
your people and your world.
As I heal, enable me to help others heal.
Amen

This first exercise in remembering your past is a simple one. It uses a basic journaling technique: list making. Sometimes the most empowering steps toward inner growth are the easiest to comprehend and the simplest to take. In this list-making exercise, you will simply itemize important elements of your life much as you would make a shopping list or a to-do list. Eventually, you will name realities that, in typical busy life, get overlooked. You can make a list of anything. For instance, you could list the key people of your childhood or the top joys of your week.

The following lists are designed to help you elicit the mighty help of memory. You may be in for some surprises. You may find that some of your happiest times are not when you got your Ph.D. or earned a promotion, but rather, as journal teacher Tristine Rainer puts it in her book *The New Diary,* "certain unexpected events in your life, an encounter with a stranger in a strange place, a moment in a play, a feeling of physical exhilaration."

The five happiest times of my childhood were when

1. _____
2. _____
3. _____
4. _____
5. _____

How did you feel before you made this list?

_____
_____
_____

How did making this list change the way you feel?

_____
_____
_____

What did you learn in making the list?

_____
_____
_____

The five happiest times of my adult life were when

1. _____
2. _____
3. _____
4. _____
5. _____

need to tell someone led me to do something that would alter my life. I picked up a composition book that cost a dollar. I soon found my composition book to be a therapist, spiritual advisor, and friend. I simply wrote out whatever was going on inside me. I wrote out my prayers. I sketched pictures to symbolize my feelings. I penned hymns of joy and poured out my fears. The book soon filled with poems, pictures, and prayers. All the bewildering newness of an adolescent spiritual awakening was sorted out in that journal.

I have kept a journal ever since. Journaling has helped seal and deepen not only my encounter with God, but also my encounter with all of life. Many adolescents have spiritual awakenings and then move on to other interests. My awakening didn't disappear, but turned into a lifelong spiritual journey. I attribute this in part to my having kept a journal. My journaling became a means of

(Continued)

seeing my inner reality clearly and taking the whole of that inner reality to a loving God for transformation.

—Robert

Did any of your answers surprise you? How?

What have you learned from these two lists about what brings you happiness?

My five outstanding talents as a child were

1.

2.

3.

4.

5.

What are your best talents now?

The five best decisions I ever made were

1.

2.

3.

4.

5.

How did you arrive at these decisions? Did you approach them the same way every time?

_____

_____

_____

My five greatest accomplishments are

1. _____

2. _____

3. _____

4. _____

5. _____

In making this list, did you find that you achieved more than you thought you had?

_____

_____

_____

Five hardships I have overcome are

1. _____

2. _____

3. _____

4. _____

5. _____

How does looking at past hardships help you deal with the difficulties you face right now?

_____

_____

_____

EXPLORING YOUR PAST WITH SYMBOLS

Another way of working with your past, of lessening the sorrow and reclaiming strength and joy, is to move from words to pictures. Journal teacher Kathleen Adams suggests making a map of the neighborhood you grew up in as a way to get in touch with your emerging story.

Draw a map of your childhood home. Feel free to add whatever details you want to add.

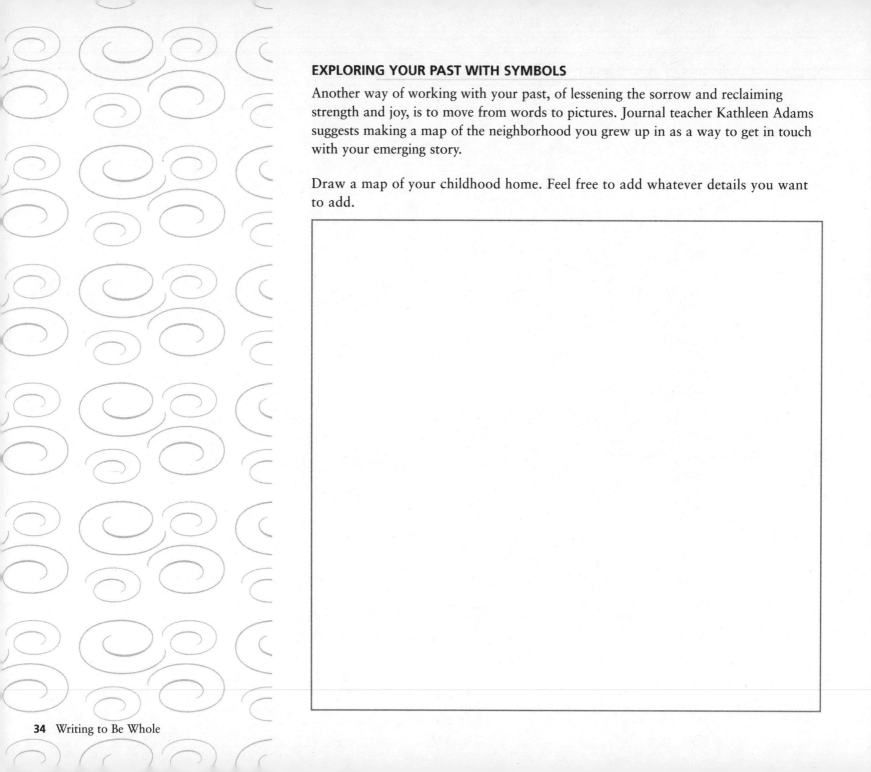

What symbols (images, sounds, and smells) emerged as you drew your map?

_____

_____

_____

What is the most joyful symbol? _____

What is the most sorrowful symbol? _____

Now map out your whole childhood neighborhood. Include whatever details are important to you—for example, certain buildings or trees.

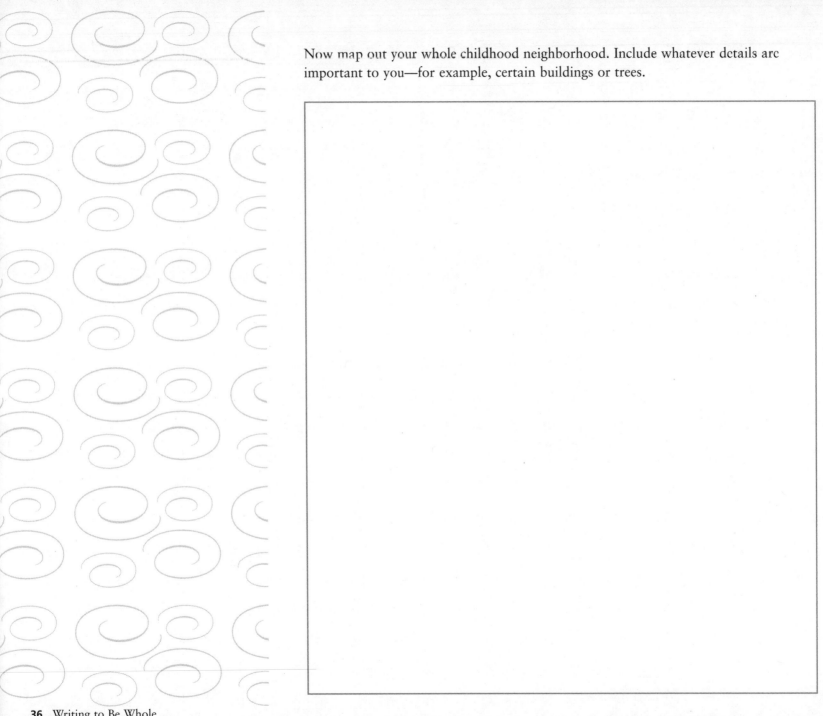

What are some of the images, sounds, and smells that emerged as you drew your neighborhood?

_____

_____

_____

What is the most joyful symbol? _____

What is the most sorrowful? _____

GIVING THANKS

Now that you have taken a special look at the blessed moments of your past, it's time to let your gratitude connect you to God. Write a prayer on the next page thanking God for all the joys of your life—the accomplishments, the learning experiences, the growth. You will not have to search hard for this prayer; it has been forming in you as you have been remembering. Let it emerge through your writing.

A PRAYER . . .
of thanks for the gifts of your past

A HEALING MOMENT

Your joys are tied to your sorrows. Whenever you remember or concentrate on your blessings, the ragged and hurtful things emerge as well. When they do, rejoice, for that nebulous, unseen pain has become recognized, named pain. Pain recognized and named is pain far closer to being healed.

Even in this joyful expedition, some hurts likely came to the surface among your joys. Name some of them.

_____

_____

_____

Right now, God is saying something to you that will ease these sorrows. Try to hear what God is saying and write it down.

_____

_____

_____

_____

_____

_____

_____

MEDITATION FOR CLOSING

Meditate on Psalm 71:5–6:

> *For you, O Lord, are my hope,*
> *my trust, O LORD, from my youth.*
> *Upon you I have leaned from my birth;*
> *it was you who took me from my mother's womb.*
> *My praise is continually of you.*

Take a few moments to write your response to this passage.

_____

_____

_____

_____

_____

_____

_____

5 Healing Your Life Story

In the last chapter, you had a chance to jog your memory and recall some of the strengths, joys, and sorrows of your life. In this chapter, you will move into a critical phase of inner healing: recovering the plot of your life.

The plot of your life is the central story of your life, the main narrative strand. That strand of narrative is moved along by stepping-stones, or "landmark events," as we call them in this book. The more you remember the landmark events in your life, the clearer the plot and the linkage between the events become. Your journal can become that place where you discover your stories. You tell your stories not only to yourself in your journal but also to God, and only in telling them to God do you truly tell them to yourself. In those stories you discover something unexpected: the heartbeat of redemption, pulsing in all the twists and turns of your personal narratives, through the major events as they unfold. Each time you tell your stories—and you can tell them in your journal many times over—they become stories that mend and transfigure your existence. You meet the sacred presence in the heart of your stories. You meet God in your stories. And because you see that your life came from somewhere and is going somewhere, each new day's reality begins to take on depth and possess the quality of "more" that we call the transcendent.

When your life malfunctions, it is often because you have lost touch with the plot of your life. This chapter will help you find and tell your story. Part of your story will be loss and sadness. But part of it will be love and accomplishment.

Through the centuries, spiritual "journalists" have used landmark events in their lives to help them plot their life stories. The biblical story was fashioned around landmark events such as creation, the enslavement of the Hebrews, and their deliverance from Egypt.

Your life has had many sacred moments—landmark events within landmark events, plots within plots. Ira Pogroff, a modern teacher of journal writing, calls these events

---

Much of my own healing came from uncovering the plot of my life. Journaling starts an inner process. Your problems begin to untangle and your soul unfurls. You can never predict what you'll run into once the process gets going.

Three years after I began my journal, my most painful memory emerged. It helped me see how my need to be fathered was a theme that formed the plot of my early life. As I journaled, I remembered a landmark event, my father's leaving for Vietnam. I remembered this while I was writing about how I had missed having a father for much of my childhood.

For the first eight years of my life, I had a wonderful relationship with my father. But all of that changed when he left to fight in Vietnam the year I turned eight. I knew that I might lose him forever. I remember the day he left. As I tried to say good-bye,

(Continued)

"stepping-stones" because they are like rocks in a stream; you move from one to the other as you make your path through the water. Richard Peace, a theologian at Fuller Seminary and another modern teacher on journal writing, calls them "hinge events."

The term *landmark events* is used here because landmarks are basic tools that help you find your way. Just as physical landmarks—a water tower on a hill, an old post office—help you find your way, landmark events help you find the plot of your life story. They are, as Kathleen Adams puts it in her book *Journal to the Self,* "the markers, the places you paused, the times when perhaps you said to yourself, 'Ah, my life will never be the same again.' . . . They are simply the markings that are significant to us as we reconstruct the movement of our life."

Landmarks do more than help you make a transition. They give your world a particular location and identity. When you think of the place where you grew up, you think of landmarks—your grammar school, a certain route through your neighborhood, a favorite tree or hill, the site of a tragedy or triumph. You think of the same types of things when you think about where you live now—your favorite coffee shop or restaurant, the best view in the area, the arena where your favorite team won a championship. Paris brings to mind the Eiffel Tower; San Francisco conjures up the Golden Gate Bridge. Physical landmarks not only help you navigate, they also give your world symbols.

"By renewing our past," Richard Peace reminds us, "we also begin to recognize the footprints of God in our life. They weren't always clear at the time but in retrospect we can see patterns."

The more you work with landmarks, the more landmarks you will find. There are landmarks within landmarks. There are landmarks in your personal life, landmarks in your spiritual life, landmarks in your work life. All these landmarks help form the intricate map of your life story. As you learn your landmarks and the increasingly complete map they make of your past, sorrows from long ago will begin to lose their sting. Joys from long ago will increase. As St. Aelred of Rievaulx put it: "a sorrow that is shared is cut in half, a joy that is shared is doubled."

When you write about your painful landmark events, you make them visible, and thus manageable. The pain you know and understand is far less fearsome than the unknown pain. The same thing happens with the joyful landmark events you write about. You can see them in their fullness, own them, and celebrate them.

And, best of all, you discover the compassionate nearness of God, your companion in the past, present, and future.

Some of your landmarks can be called major transition points. The major transition points are the obvious significant events of your life. These can include your birth, your first day of school or your graduation from school, your marriage, the birth of your children, the death of someone close to you. Remember that you are writing not only for your own eyes but for God's eyes as well. You write in God's presence and with God's guidance. In this atmosphere you will uncover the plot of your life.

In this chapter, you will

- make a list of the landmarks in your life

- write stories about your landmarks

- write prayers about what your lists and stories bring to the surface of your life

PRAYER OF ENTRANCE

Merciful and loving God,
you are nearer than my heartbeat,
closer than my breath.
Help me in my remembering,
for you are the holder of my steps
and the keeper of my story.
You remember when I forget.
I choose to remember in your presence
and I ask your guidance in my writing,
that I may see how you guided me
in all the turnings and windings of my life.
Amen

can fill my need." Then I said to God, "I missed having a father. I need you to be my father." I sensed God saying, "Robert, that is all I have ever wanted to do."

God began to fill that hole in my heart. Then the fresh memories of the good times I had had with my father emerged. I not only discovered in new ways my heavenly Father, but I began to enjoy a new, healthy relationship with my earthly father. I pulled out my journal, and as I wrote, many of the landmark events of joy with my father poured out. The scenes of pain and joy helped me plot my relationship with my father.

—Robert

THE MAJOR LANDMARKS OF YOUR LIFE

Now that you have given yourself to God for this period of writing, it is time to list the major transition points in your life. Write out as many as twelve. Remember that you can come back to this list if you discover landmark events you left out the first time.

1. **I was born**
2. _____
3. _____
4. _____
5. _____
6. _____
7. _____
8. _____
9. _____
10. _____
11. _____
12. _____

Now that you have listed your major transition points, it's time to write the stories that go with these transitions. These stories are within you. Writing them out, telling them to yourself and to God, will help you heal.

You will have space to write the stories of up to five of your major transition points. You might want to do all five at once, or you may choose to do one or two, then go on to other parts of the journal and return later to finish your stories. You may even want to pull out an additional notebook and write stories on all of your major transition points.

Be sure to include the story of your birth (or your adoption) in your five stories. You have likely heard the details about how long the delivery took, who was present, and where the hospital was located. The different accounts you have heard from relatives and friends will blend into your story of your birth. Telling that story will help you contact the love others have felt for you. Sometimes writing such accounts can help you contact your sorrows as well, bringing them to the surface.

After you have told the story of your birth, pick four more transition points from the list you just made and write stories about them. Kathleen Adams suggests beginning the stories of your landmark events with the phrase "It was a time when . . ."

LANDMARK EVENT 1
The story of my birth

_____

_____

_____

_____

_____

_____

_____

_____

_____

_____

_____

_____

LANDMARK EVENT 2
The story of _____

LANDMARK EVENT 3
The story of _____

_____

_____

_____

_____

_____

_____

_____

_____

_____

_____

_____

_____

_____

_____

_____

LANDMARK EVENT 4
The story of _____

_____
_____
_____
_____
_____
_____
_____
_____
_____
_____
_____
_____
_____
_____
_____
_____
_____
_____
_____
_____

LANDMARK EVENT 5
The story of

TAKING YOUR STORIES TO GOD

Often a catharsis, a cleansing, occurs when you put your stories on paper. You may cry or laugh. Or you may have to stop writing and just rest in the stillness.

Now that you have written one or more stories, it is time to turn to God with the feelings that emerged from your expedition into the past. You can take the sorrow, as well as the gratitude, to God.

A PRAYER . . .
for healing the sorrows of my life story

Take a moment of stillness to get in touch with any sorrows and regrets that came to you in your writing and then complete the following prayer.

Compassionate, all-merciful, all-loving God,
Here are some of the sorrows and regrets that emerged in my story:

_____

_____

_____

_____

_____

_____

_____

_____

_____

_____

_____

_____

_____

_____

God replies with these healing words:

_____
_____
_____
_____
_____
_____
_____
_____
_____
_____
_____
_____
_____
_____
_____
_____
_____
_____

Gratitude—for God's presence, for creation, for the people in your life—can also emerge when you tell your life story. In your own words, write a prayer of thanks to God.

A PRAYER . . .
of gratitude

_____

_____

_____

_____

_____

_____

_____

_____

_____

_____

_____

_____

_____

MEDITATION FOR CLOSING

Meditate on Psalm 139:13–18 (NAB):

> *You formed my inmost being;*
>   *you knit me in my mother's womb.*
> *I praise you, so wonderfully you made me;*
>   *wonderful are your works!*
> *My very self you knew;*
>   *my bones were not hidden from you,*
> *When I was being made in secret,*
>   *fashioned as in the depths of the earth.*
> *Your eyes foresaw my actions;*
>   *in your book all are written down;*
>   *my days were shaped, before one came to be.*
> *How precious to me are your designs, O God;*
>   *how vast the sum of them!*
> *Were I to count, they would outnumber the sands;*
>   *to finish, I would need eternity.*

Take a few moments to write your response to this passage.

6 *Healing Past Relationships*

In the last chapter, you looked at the plot of your life and began to see how different parts of your history fit together. Your next task is to explore past relationships.

Nothing in life can surpass the exquisite joy of human relationships. You may have known moments when your relationships have passed over into the sacred. Perhaps after a long day with family and friends, boating on the lake or playing touch football, everyone settles in as evening comes. You are pleasantly exhausted. Time stops. In the presence of those you love, eternity breaks in. Light, shadow, sound, smell, and sight all seem hallowed. You are present to those you love, and God is in your midst. Perhaps such a moment comes after listening to your grandparents tell stories about earlier times. You can also touch a bit of eternity during moments with your husband or wife and your children. In these moments the holy filters in, transfiguring reality for a while. Even the stillness after a quarrel, when tears, forgiveness, and quiet have restored love, can have a place in your album of holy memories.

But not all the moments you have shared with people have come close to the sacred. You have swallowed your bitterness when charity turned to hostility. You've seen a friendship end in cold anger. You and the other person were never able to bring the problem into the open, talk about it, and resolve your conflict. After a while, your insides turned to ice.

You have likely been surprised by betrayal and abuse. You have faced destructive rage in others; maybe you have become full of rage yourself. Maybe you have actively hated someone, intending to harm and not to heal.

You have lost important people to death, illness, and divorce. Sometimes the loss had to do with wrongdoing, but sometimes each person was a victim of circumstance, and the loss couldn't be helped.

One of the most powerful stories I know about healed relationships is the story of George.

When I met George at a parish prayer meeting twenty-three years ago, the first thing I noticed about him was a look of devotion and joy that seemed to make him glow. He was what many would call a natural mystic. He drew close to God through long periods of daily contemplative prayer. When he spoke of God's love in his life, God's presence seemed tangible. At that time, I was unaware of the horror that George faced at home, a horror that would begin often as soon as he got home after the prayer meeting. Years later I would learn that George's father had sexually abused him for about ten years.

I lost touch with George in the early eighties, and my next contact with him was a phone conversation in 1988. At the time, an

(Continued)

AIDS patient was being profiled in the news, and though they tried to hide his identity, I figured out that it was George. He confirmed this when I called him up to ask about the story.

George was married now and had three children. The profile had mentioned that he'd contracted AIDS through promiscuous, high-risk behavior. I couldn't make any sense of it. How could such a devoted young man—and a loving family man—end up like this?

George explained that his father had raped him for years and that even after he was able to break free from his father, he was unable to break those dangerous patterns of behavior. Promiscuous, secretive, and high-risk sex had become his compulsion. It seemed that the behavior his father had subjected him to had in some way shaped George.

However, in spite of what his father had done, and in spite of his father's continued inability to take responsibility for the abuse
(Continued)

It's also quite possible that your soul was badly hurt by abuse or neglect during childhood, and now, as an adult, you have little capacity to enter richly into relationships.

If you suffered abuse as a child, you might have been silenced by an unwritten rule in your family: Don't express your feelings. You might have grown up believing that, as psychotherapist Terry Vance puts it, "mistakes are irrevocable." Vance goes on to say that children raised in abusive families "become secretive adults who mask their feelings by hiding them or pretending to have feelings they do not have. But masks harm, even deaden the person underneath."

Some people believe in tackling fractured relationships head-on. However, it can be helpful to take a gentler approach. Rather than simply digging up past pain in relationships, it is often more effective to start with the good feelings and then inch your way back toward those deeply entrenched feelings of conflict.

As you recall the good times with people, the pain of fractured relationships will emerge on its own. Through the exercises in this chapter, you will have an opportunity to take that pain to Jesus.

Journaling allows you to express your worst anger and hurt in a way that is safe for you and for others. You might think of the journal page as a canvas at which you can throw your raw emotions. In your journal you can replay situations. As you prayerfully write out your recollections, you may find that you can see them in a more objective way. You may see what you might have contributed to the pain or misunderstanding. You may begin to see possible strategies for reconciliation. You may gather the courage to ask for forgiveness or to talk with the other person more calmly, without getting defensive or feeling vengeful.

Journaling might help you see another person as God sees him or her. You may actually see God in that person, even though he or she injured you. You can thus learn to love in a sacrificial way, by casting your ego at the feet of the person or persons with whom you are called to be in a relationship.

How can journaling these hurts make such a difference? When you write out your experiences and feelings, you give them a form, where before they were in a jumbled, chaotic state. Once they have a shape and you can recognize them, you can turn them over to God. Psychologist James Pennebaker, in his book *Opening Up: The Healing Power of Expressing Emotions*, says, "Writing about traumas helps organize traumas, thereby freeing the mind to deal with other tasks."

In this chapter, you will

- remember and write about the times when you felt loved

- envision some of the people who best loved and affirmed you in the past

- allow memories to strengthen your ability to love and forgive in the present

PRAYER OF ENTRANCE

Merciful, strong, and tender God,
I inch slowly into the cathedral of the holy;
I move a bit at a time into the core of my soul.
I know that at times your love has
been transmitted to me by
flesh-and-blood human beings
who embodied your caring.
The love of the one Savior has come
through many fallible human helpers.
I have also known loss in my relationships.
Loved ones have died.
Close friends and family have grown distant.
I have experienced the hurt of
bitter words and hostile actions.
Throughout the pattern of my relationships,
you call out to me; you love me.
I take to you both the sacred and the
painful parts of my relationships,
that you may touch, heal, and restore them.
Amen

(he actually blamed George), George wanted reconciliation with his father. The doctors predicted that George had very little time left, and what George wanted more than anything was to reconcile with the man who had harmed him. He desperately wanted his father to accept the unconditional forgiveness George wanted to offer. George wanted to end the estrangement and allow healing to come into the relationship. He had already worked on healing himself with the help of a counselor. He had already acknowledged his rage toward his father. He was ready now to bring his father into the healing process.

George suffered for the next few years. His disease moved frighteningly fast. He was visited by fevers and racked with pain in his joints and muscles. He received special grace through his wife, who, though angry and heartsick, never left his side. His only son, aged nine, also stayed with him.

(Continued)

As George faded and his mind moved in and out of delirium, he continued to pursue his father. But his father could not bring himself, even in the face of impending loss, to be reconciled. To be reconciled with someone you have hurt, you have to first admit what you have done. Instead, George's father bellowed at him and actually accused George of wanting the sexual relationship (his father could not even call it abuse). Each time I visited George, he would say that he was not going to give up on his father.

Then one day it happened. George finally broke through to his father. They cried together, and his father accepted at last the pleadings of an unrelenting son who cared more about reconciliation than blame, more about healing than fault or guilt. George never blamed his father for his own dangerous infidelities or for the resulting illness. He needed only to forgive his father and have his father take responsibility for

(Continued)

CONFRONTING THE SACRED IN RELATIONSHIPS

An essential step in confronting the pain in relationships is confronting the strengths and joys in your history of relationships. When you're in pain, it's easy to push away the memories of the good and joyful aspects of your relationships. So the beginning of healing is often the intentional recalling of what worked well in your relationships. Fiercely taking possession of the strengths that your relationships have brought you will build you up and help you feel safe and secure enough to confront the unfinished business you have with others.

Earlier in this book you used lists to help you focus and to help your thoughts become visible. You will now use lists to help you remember your relationships.

The times I felt loved growing up were when

1. _____

2. _____

3. _____

4. _____

5. _____

From the times you listed, pick the most sacred and write the story of that time.

_____

_____

_____

_____

_____

_____

_____

_____

_____

_____

_____

_____

_____

_____

_____

_____

_____

_____

the terrible wrong that had been done to him.

When I visited George shortly before his death, I saw that his spiritual glow had returned. Triumph and joy now thrived despite the waste caused by the disease. He told me about the new closeness between him and his father. Now George could die in peace. _Yes_, I thought, _and now so can your father; you have helped save his soul._

George taught me more about reconciliation, forgiveness, and the healing that is possible in relationships than my theology studies ever could. Even in his earlier years, George was determined to love his abusive father, and this desire was based upon the radical love God had shown George.

Not everyone who has been abused as severely as George should confront his or her abuser. Sometimes such confrontation causes more hurt than healing. But in George's case it was the

(Continued)

right thing to do. The choice to confront and forgive in the way George did is always deeply personal. George chose to confront and forgive for the sake of his adult brothers and sisters. Only when his father admitted the full horror of the wrong could the whole family stop denying the awful truth and get on with life. And only forgiveness, freely offered by George, could bring his father to the place of admitting the truth.

The prevailing opinion in our society is often this: When a relationship hurts, it is best to just leave. But people such as George give us a different message: Don't run from the pain, but walk through it until you come to a place of healing, a place of glory. It is a difficult route, but it is the only one that will make us whole.

—Robert

What did you feel as you wrote the story?

Did God seem present as you wrote? If so, in what way?

AN IMAGE OF A TIME YOU FELT LOVED

The significant moments of your life will become potent with meaning when you allow them to become symbols. Once, in late fall, I (Robert) made a bicycle trip with three friends to the Smoky Mountains. The evening we reached the mountains, the sky was clear and brilliant. We pulled our bikes onto the side of the road so we could rest and warm ourselves with coffee from the thermos. We could see the dim shape of the mountains and the lights of the valley below us. We didn't speak. God was present in the sheer stillness of our souls as we surveyed that scene. Years later, when I journaled about that moment, I drew a picture of a bike with a coffee thermos strapped on it. The picture, even more than words, vividly etched that moment on my soul. This picture became my symbol of a time when I met God with others. When I thumb through my journal now, just looking at the picture evokes that moment with God and my friends.

Quickly sketch a picture that symbolizes the time you felt most loved.

A GUIDED MEDITATION: YOU STRENGTHEN THE CAPACITY FOR LOVING

Get comfortable and ready to imagine . . .

You are sitting in your dining room. Jesus comes to you. He says, "There have been people in your life who have loved you well, who could see the beauty within you and the sacredness of your personality. These people had a knack for affirming you. Would you name five of those people for me?"

The people who best affirmed me are

1. _____

I picked this person because

_____

_____

2. _____

I picked this person because

_____

_____

_____

3. _____

I picked this person because

_____

_____

_____

4. _____

I picked this person because

_____

_____

_____

5. _____

I picked this person because

_____

_____

_____

Jesus now asks you to follow him into your living room. You find the five people you just listed standing there. One by one, each of them takes your hand or embraces you. Jesus asks you to sit in a chair in the middle of the room. The five people gather around you. Each of the five people quietly places a hand on your head or shoulder, and the whole group prays for you silently.

What images, sensations, and memories reveal themselves during this prayer?

_____

_____

_____

Each person sees in you a unique beauty. One by one they tell you of the beauty and giftedness they see.

PERSON 1: _____

"I love you and find you beautiful because

_____

_____

_____

"I see these gifts within you:

_____

_____

_____

PERSON 2: _____

"I love you and find you beautiful because

_____

_____

"I see these gifts within you:

_____

_____

_____

PERSON 3: _____

"I love you and find you beautiful because

_____

_____

_____

"I see these gifts within you:

_____

_____

_____

PERSON 4: _____

"I love you and find you beautiful because

_____

_____

_____

"I see these gifts within you:

_____

_____

_____

PERSON 5: _____

"I love you and find you beautiful because

_____

_____

_____

"I see these gifts within you:

_____

_____

_____

TALKING WITH JESUS ABOUT THE PAINS OF YOUR RELATIONSHIPS

Whenever you remember the holy and joyful aspects of your relationships, the hurt and the loss come to mind too. Your finest loves on this earth are impermanent, and even the best relationships have their ragged spots. No one can guarantee that death and illness will not separate you from those you hold dear.

When you remember the beauty of some relationships, it is inevitable that you will remember the breakdown of other relationships.

Regrets also are likely to emerge. When you remember the times you felt loved, you will often remember the times you didn't give thanks to others and the times you neglected or hurt others.

Use the rest of this page to talk with Jesus about any hurts and regrets that emerged during this chapter.

_____

_____

_____

_____

_____

_____

_____

_____

_____

_____

_____

_____

_____

_____

_____

_____

_____

_____

_____

_____

MEDITATION FOR CLOSING

Meditate on 1 John 4:7–12:

> *Beloved, let us love one another, because love is from God; everyone who loves is born of God and knows God. Whoever does not love does not know God, for God is love. God's love was revealed among us in this way: God sent his only Son into the world so that we might live through him. In this is love, not that we loved God but that he loved us and sent his Son to be the atoning sacrifice for our sins. Beloved, since God loved us so much, we also ought to love one another. No one has ever seen God; if we love one another, God lives in us, and his love is perfected in us.*

Take a few moments to write your response to this passage.

7 *Journeying with St. Hildegard*

Your journaling has taken you on a pilgrimage through the past. You have looked at the sacred moments of your history, confronted the painful relationships, and taken the pain to God. You can now begin healing the present.

In this chapter, you will use an ancient Christian healing technique: the guided meditation. Dante's *Divine Comedy* is a medieval example of a guided meditation. The reader follows Dante through hell and purgatory to finally reach the beatific vision. Bonaventure's long guided-vision journey, *Lignum Vitae* (*The Tree of Life*), is another wonderful example. The reader follows, through a series of guided visualizations, the life of Christ to a profoundly transfiguring closing in which the reader is bathed in the fountain of light that comes from the heart of God.

Throughout the centuries, particularly at high-water points in faith, such as the period from 1050 to 1350, pilgrims journeyed by the thousands to healing shrines throughout Europe. They walked to these shrines seeking healing of body or soul. Traveling in groups, they told their stories to one another and prayed together as they walked. They engaged in a practice known as visionary incubation, disposing their hearts to visions as they traveled and once they arrived at the shrine. They spent their nights sleeping on the floors of the shrines and their days praying and "incubating," making their hearts ready for healing visions that often occurred at daybreak after days of prayer. Thousands of firsthand accounts of these visions and healings have been passed on to us. In ordinary life, Christians such as St. Thomas Aquinas would seek moments of visionary enlightenment to help them understand Scripture and faith.

This chapter takes guided meditation and combines it with journaling. The visions you will write about can heal your wounds.

It took nearly a millennium, but Hildegard's writings have finally hit the best-seller lists. After being all but forgotten for hundreds of years, Hildegard's life and work are attracting people from all walks of life.

This isn't surprising. Hildegard was a wonderfully creative human being. A strong-willed, deeply spiritual woman, she used imagery, poetry, music, and powerful prose to describe the reality of human life met by God's grace. She preached all over Europe, boldly advising priests and bishops when she felt they needed it. She was a great musician, and her hymns, newly recorded, have today found an enthusiastic audience. She possessed a special gift for the mending of souls, and people made pilgrimages from countries all over Europe to experience the healing power of her presence.

—Eddie

In this chapter, you will

- go on a pilgrimage with St. Hildegard of Bingen

- choose traveling companions to help you on your journey

- describe your life through symbols, pictures, and visions

- create scenes that will help you move toward personal change

PRAYER OF ENTRANCE

Dear God,
you hold together my past and my present.
You are the one who can knit together
all the parts of my soul, making me whole.
I give this time of journaling to you.
Guide my steps along this pilgrimage.
May I meet you in awe and wonder.
May I find you in the daily stuff of my living.
I give my past to you.
I offer you my present.
I place my world, inside and out, into your hands.
Amen

A GUIDED MEDITATION: YOU GO ON A PILGRIMAGE

Get comfortable and ready to imagine . . .

You find yourself outside a convent. Its slender spires reach toward heaven. It's an enchantingly beautiful day. A few fluffy clouds drift across a sky of vivid blue.

The doors of the convent open, and out comes Hildegard, striding toward you with powerful, graceful steps. On her arm she is holding a cloth-covered basket.

"We are going on a pilgrimage, one that will transform you. You are back in my time, the time you call the Middle Ages. You may think of it as a period full of trouble.

Well, we have our problems. But it is also a time of great creativity and imagination, a time when talented women like me can be an important force in society and the church.

"It is also a time of rich humanity, a time of stories, visions, and wonders. In this time people make pilgrimages to saints' shrines for healing, rejuvenation, insight, and transformation. These pilgrimages are part religious event, part vacation. People often make their pilgrimages with groups of people rather than alone.

"When they go on pilgrimages, they expect mending, usually of the body, but often of the soul as well. Pilgrims ready their hearts for visions and insights by praying with each other along the way and telling each other stories. They arrive at the shrine and pray there day and night, sleeping in the shrine. Often, usually at daybreak, they have a vision that brings healing and realization.

"Today, you and I are going on a pilgrimage.

"First, I have a present for you. You possess gifts, special graces God has given you. These are inner graces such as wisdom and gentleness, the ability to console, the ability to speak in ways that touch the heart. Sometimes these gifts lie dormant inside you, undiscovered. They are gifts you have not yet fully known or used. God has gifted you, and now is the time for you to discover one of your gifts. It will be a gift for you to develop, with God's help.

"I hold in this basket, covered by cloth, an item that symbolizes a yet undiscovered gift within you. When you are ready, you can remove the cover of the basket and view the item that symbolizes the gift. You can remove the cloth now and view the item."

You lift the cloth and look inside the basket.

Hildegard smiles at you and asks, "What item do you see in the basket?"

Quickly sketch a picture of the item.

Hildegard asks, "What gift does the item symbolize?"

Write your response.

_____

_____

_____

Hildegard asks, "What difference do you think accepting and using this gift can make in your life and in the lives of those you love?"

Write your response.

_____

_____

_____

Hildegard asks, "What can you do to nurture this gift?"

Write your response.

_____

_____

_____

"Now," Hildegard says, "it is time to plan our pilgrimage. The healing shrines are usually dedicated to saints, especially those saints that possess healing gifts. You will pick the saint whose shrine you will visit. It does not matter if there is not a physical shrine built for the saint you choose. We are journeying in the landscape of the soul, and in the landscape of the soul, all saints can have shrines.

"It is important to pick a holy person who possessed a special gift for healing hearts. You may pick an actual Catholic saint, such as St. Francis, St. Teresa of Ávila, or Padre Pio. Or you can pick a holy person, such as Mother Teresa of Calcutta, who is not an 'official' saint, or someone like John Wesley, who is not even Catholic. Pick someone who evokes for you God's nearness.

"What person do you choose?" _____

"What draws you to this person?"

_____

_____

_____

"What about this person reminds you of God?"

_____

_____

_____

CHOOSING FOUR COMPANIONS FOR THE PILGRIMAGE

Hildegard continues: "Now that you have picked your saint, it is time to pick your companions. Besides me, you can have four companions. These should be people you know, or know about, who can help you on your journey. These four companions may be people who are close to you, but they can also be people who have influenced you from a distance, such as John Paul II, Billy Graham, or Rosa Parks. Use your imagination. Who has the ability to say just the right thing to inspire you, comfort you, and help you grow?"

YOUR FIRST COMPANION . . .
can see into your soul

The first companion you choose for your pilgrimage should be a person who has a special gift of insight, someone who can look at your expression and see into your soul. Even though this person possesses the gift of being able to look inside people's souls, he or she does so in a way that helps, not hurts.

Whom do you choose? _____

You now look toward the door of the convent, and this person comes out and stands beside you and Hildegard. You look this person in the eye and explain why you chose him or her.

_____

_____

_____

_____

_____

_____

_____

_____

_____

_____

_____

_____

YOUR SECOND COMPANION . . .
can console and heal you

This person should be a "tear catcher," someone who can say just the right word or make just the right gesture to help you.

Whom do you choose? _____

You look toward the door of the convent, and this person comes out and stands beside you and Hildegard. You look this person in the eye and explain why you chose him or her.

_____

_____

_____

_____

_____

_____

_____

_____

_____

_____

_____

_____

_____

_____

YOUR THIRD COMPANION . . .
can challenge you to change

The spiritual journey is about far more than being comforted and inspired; it is also about experiencing change. You change in order to become more like the person God wants you to become—more loving, more centered on others, more in tune with Scripture. You could say that you are called to holiness. Sometimes you can become mired in destructive patterns that hurt you and also hurt God. Addictions of all sorts can impair your ability to love and serve. Sin is not a popular word, but sin can trap you in selfishness, preventing you from offering to others the gift of who you are.

This third companion should be someone who can challenge you to change, not in a way that degrades you, but in a way that makes change possible.

Whom do you choose? _____

You look toward the door of the convent, and this person comes out and stands beside you and Hildegard. You look this person in the eye and explain why you chose him or her.

YOUR FOURTH COMPANION . . .
can inspire you

This should be someone who can help you envision unthought-of possibilities, arouse in you enthusiasm for the future, energize you with hope, and make God vivid and alive to you.

Whom do you choose? _____

You look toward the door of the convent, and this person comes out and stands beside you and Hildegard. You look this person in the eye and explain why you chose him or her.

_____

_____

_____

_____

_____

_____

_____

_____

_____

_____

_____

_____

SETTING FOOT ON THE PATHWAY

You, Hildegard, and your four companions join hands in silent prayer to begin this, your pilgrimage of transformation. They ask you to utter a short prayer to bless the journey. Write your prayer here.

_____

_____

_____

You start off, and the day is beautiful. You sing together. Name one of the songs you sing.

_____

Toward evening, tiredness overcomes you. Your muscles ache. You look up and see that the sky has become filled with gray and black clouds. First a little rain and then a torrent pours down on you. Jagged lightening flashes. Thunder booms so loudly that the earth shakes. The once bright day has turned wild and ferocious. The cold wetness soaks through to your skin. You see a barn nearby, and you all run to it, enter, and find spots in the hay where you can rest. You shiver miserably from the cold. You and your first companion, _____, the one who can see into your soul, cover yourselves with hay for warmth as you huddle in a corner of the barn.

The brightness of the day is gone. All the difficulties of your life crash in on you. Worry knots your stomach. You are assaulted by those ever-present, inner aches.

Your companion, _____, looks at you for a long moment and then speaks. "I see a tumult inside you. Tell me about it."

You pause, swallow hard, and tell _____ about the tumult of your soul.

_____

_____

_____

_____

_____

_____

_____

_____

_____ listens to you kindly and attentively. "I see more in your soul,"

_____ tells you, "more than you have been willing to tell me. This is

what I see:

_____

_____

_____

"I see a deep hurt that you have never fully told anyone about. It is this:

_____

_____

_____

Your companion continues. "Often on pilgrimages, people have visions at night that vividly depict their problems in a way that helps them understand their problems more clearly. You may have such a vision tonight."

You are tired. Your clothes are nearly dry now, and the warm hay is lulling you to sleep. Your talk with your companion has helped lift some weight from your soul.

You are in a deep sleep now. You see a brightness that surely comes from angels, heralding a solemn and holy vision in a dream to come. You begin dreaming a vivid, clear dream that depicts the origins and nature of the central problem your companion _____ perceived when he or she looked into your soul.

Your vision reveals scenes that depict a core difficulty in your life. Consciously invent, imagine, and then write a vision scene that would make vivid this central difficulty. Usually people begin by imagining the first part of the vision, and then they find that soon after their pen touches the page, their creative forces flow and the visionary scene just pours out from heart to hand to page. Use this same method for the other vision scenes in this book. Write your vision here.

You awaken and rub your eyes. You smell breakfast cooking on a fire just outside the barn's entrance. You gather with your other companions, and you all share the meal. Your companions chat amiably as they eat. You find it hard to enter into their conversation. Your mind ruminates over the events of the night, the core problem that became clear in your conversation with _____.

_____, the companion you chose because of his or her special ability to comfort, comes up to you and places a hand on your shoulder. "I see that you're troubled. I'll walk beside you on the day's journey."

All of you gather before leaving, join hands, and sing a song that is comforting to you. What is the song? _____

_____, your companion who has the special ability to comfort, walks beside you on the day's journey. As the two of you walk along the road, you tell him or her about your core difficulty, the one that is becoming so clear to you. Your companion looks at you for a moment. There are tears in _____'s eyes. As you walk together this day, _____ speaks words that give you encouragement and comfort. They are the kindhearted words you have longed to hear all your life. Here are those words:

_____

_____

_____

_____

_____

_____

_____

_____

_____ now gives you these suggestions for mending your core difficulty:

_____

_____

_____

A COMFORTING VISION TO MEND THE SOUL

By now it is afternoon. Everyone has grown tired from the journey. Hildegard and one of your companions spread blankets on the grass at the roadside.

You lie down and quickly fall asleep. In the depths of this pleasant afternoon sleep, a vision comes to you in a dream.

In the first part of your dream, you are carried to the place that is for you the safest and most comforting. This location holds a special place in your memory. In your dream, the light of God's presence shines throughout every part of this location.

Describe this place that holds special meaning for you, this place in which you feel safe.

_____

_____

_____

Describe how it looks with God's light surrounding it.

_____

_____

_____

Why is this place so comforting to you?

_____

_____

_____

A scene now unfolds, bringing a degree of resolution to your deepest problem. This scene places God's ease in your soul's recesses.

Describe this scene.

_____

_____

_____

_____

_____

_____

_____

_____

You awaken and see Hildegard. She asks you to quickly draw a sketch that will symbolize the vision you just had. As soon as you touch your pen or pencil to paper, a picture that symbolizes your vision will begin to form. Sketch that picture here.

As you begin walking again, your third companion, _____, walks beside you. This is the companion who can challenge you to change. This companion senses the ease that has come over you. _____ tells you, "God brings you comfort so that you can comfort others. The call of the gospel is a call to spend your life caring for those God cares for, especially the poor and rejected. Following God means opening your heart so that God may change it. Following God means always moving in directions that give life to others. Change means clearing up the inconsistencies in your life, facing the addictions, and looking boldly at your self-centeredness. In what ways do you think you need to change?"

Write your response.

_____

_____

_____

_____

_____

_____

_____

Your third companion now says, "I have a special gift for sensing how people need to change. I think the most important change you need in your life is

_____

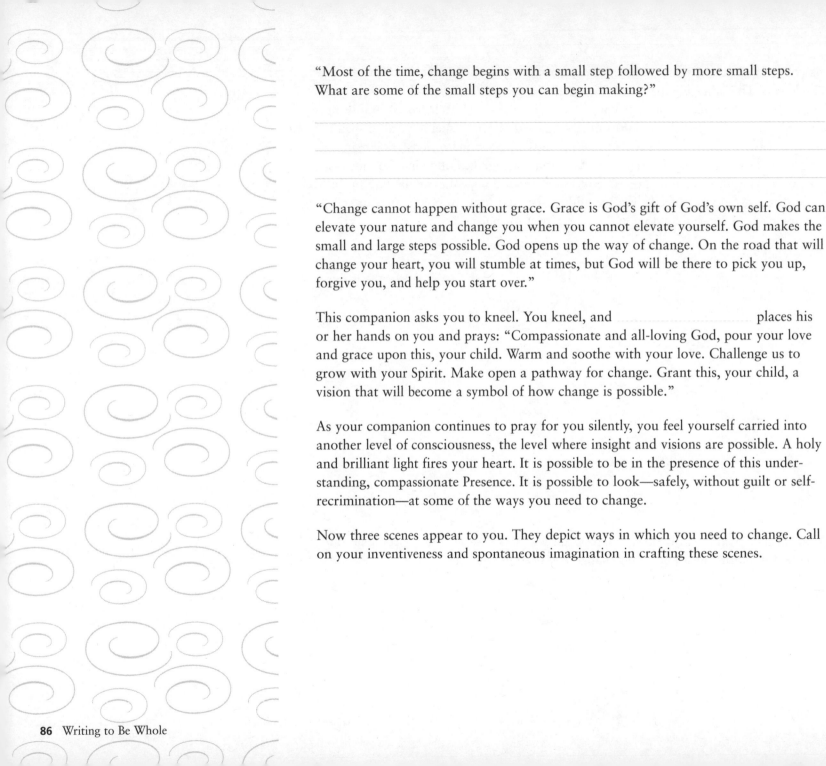

"Most of the time, change begins with a small step followed by more small steps. What are some of the small steps you can begin making?"

_____

_____

_____

"Change cannot happen without grace. Grace is God's gift of God's own self. God can elevate your nature and change you when you cannot elevate yourself. God makes the small and large steps possible. God opens up the way of change. On the road that will change your heart, you will stumble at times, but God will be there to pick you up, forgive you, and help you start over."

This companion asks you to kneel. You kneel, and _____ places his or her hands on you and prays: "Compassionate and all-loving God, pour your love and grace upon this, your child. Warm and soothe with your love. Challenge us to grow with your Spirit. Make open a pathway for change. Grant this, your child, a vision that will become a symbol of how change is possible."

As your companion continues to pray for you silently, you feel yourself carried into another level of consciousness, the level where insight and visions are possible. A holy and brilliant light fires your heart. It is possible to be in the presence of this understanding, compassionate Presence. It is possible to look—safely, without guilt or self-recrimination—at some of the ways you need to change.

Now three scenes appear to you. They depict ways in which you need to change. Call on your inventiveness and spontaneous imagination in crafting these scenes.

SCENE 1

SCENE 2

SCENE 3

Now a final scene unfolds, depicting a series of small steps, little beginnings you can make on the road to change. What are some of those steps?

_____

_____

_____

_____

_____

_____

_____

_____

You hear an utterly holy and noble voice, a voice that embodies both love and majesty. It is the voice of God. You hear God speak words to you that will enable you to change. Those words are:

_____

_____

_____

_____

_____

_____

_____

_____

_____

After your vision has ended, you feel a lightness of heart. You have been able to face the ways you need to change without feeling the paralyzing guilt that often accompanies such insight. There is great release in knowing that small steps are usually best and that the kind and assuring presence of the one who loves you without condition is with you always.

As you walk, you see on the horizon the spires of your shrine, the shrine dedicated to _____, the holy person you chose.

You begin to think about the qualities of the holy person you chose. Some of those qualities are

_____

_____

_____

Your fourth companion, _____, comes up to you. "I have a special gift for helping people dream of what might be. Without dreams of future possibilities, people falter. Such dreams richly paint your life goal, helping you achieve what you never thought you could achieve. Your dreams carry you up to the next horizon of life. Life grows stale without the goals and purposes that dreams can bring."

Your companion continues, "I have a thought that will inspire you. You picked _____ as your saint because you admire this person greatly. Usually the people you greatly admire embody traits and qualities that you also possess, although you may not fully realize it.

"How are you like the person you picked as your saint?"

_____

_____

_____

You companion continues: "God has truly gifted you. When a person walks with God, unthought-of possibilities become realized. Tonight, when you sleep at the shrine, you will dream a dream of what might be. In such dreams, unimagined possibilities for your life can come alive. Scenes that give your life goals and purpose will unfold."

You arrive at the shrine and see a throng of people entering it. You enter just as night falls. The cathedral has no pews, so people lie on mats on the floor. Together they sing this song:

_____

Time passes quickly. Your companion puts out a mat for you, and soon you are in a deep sleep. You begin to dream, and in your dream, the shrine is flooded with light. You hear angels singing, and then you see them.

Describe the songs and voices of the angels. How do the angels look?

_____

_____

_____

In the midst of such a holy presence, scenes unfold that depict possibilities for your life and the purpose of your life. These scenes inspire and invigorate you.

Describe some of these scenes.

_____

_____

_____

_____

_____

_____

_____

_____

_____

_____

_____

_____

_____

You wake up, and it's morning. The bells of the cathedral clang loudly with a great gladness. You offer a prayer of thanks to God.

A PRAYER . . .
of thanks

MEDITATION FOR CLOSING

Meditate on Psalm 118:29:

> *O give thanks to the* LORD, *for he is good,*
> *for his steadfast love endures forever.*

Take a few moments to write your response to this verse.

_____

_____

_____

_____

_____

_____

_____

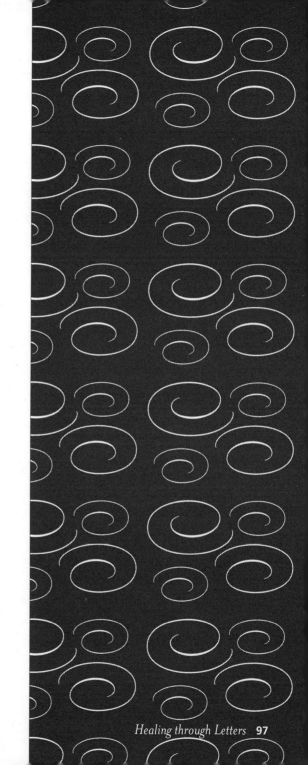

8 *Healing through Letters*

In the last chapter, you went on a pilgrimage and experienced visions that helped heal your pain and point out new horizons for your life. In this chapter, you will deal with issues in your current relationships, as well as memories from your past relationships that affect how you live now and how you relate to people in the present moment.

Most traumas involve relationships. Most healing involves facing the pain of those relationships.

You may think, as many people do, that it's better simply to move on and put troubled relationships behind you. But unless your feelings about those troubled relationships are resolved, they will remain with you, under the surface, taking your energy and interrupting your everyday consciousness when you least expect it.

While you may not be able to resolve the problems that have caused your feelings, you can move on by merely expressing those feelings. University of Texas psychologist James Pennebaker, in his book *Opening Up,* puts it this way: "The feelings are there anyway. You might as well go ahead and write to work through them."

Writing about your painful relationships can whittle that pain down to a manageable size. It will no longer loom so large. And when you write out your feelings, you can view yourself more clearly. Writing allows you to test solutions on paper when solutions are possible. It allows you to grieve, let go, and move on when solutions are not possible.

In this chapter, you will

- write guided letters to people with whom you are in conflict

- participate in a short guided meditation to deal with hurts that surface during the letter writing

PRAYER OF ENTRANCE

Loving and all-caring God,
Christ was your letter to humanity,
to all of creation.
Christ was your message, your word.
You heal us, restore us, and make life brand new
through this message, this word.
I am about to write some letters.
Please use them to heal me
and to open new pathways.
May my words, my letters,
reflect your eternal message.
Guide my prayer and my writing
as I continue this journey of healing.
Amen

WRITING LETTERS YOU MIGHT NEVER SEND

One of the best means of finding your buried feelings, expressing them, and moving beyond them is writing letters you don't plan to send, at least in the initial drafts. In such letters, you can say what you have longed to say. You can write out in vivid detail all the intensities of your emotions and put on paper the tangle of your thoughts. These letters are for your healing. But healing is only possible when you make your pain visible. Letters you may never send can help you do that.

Except for letters of gratitude, the cardinal rule of such letters is that they remain unsent in the initial drafts. They should only be sent after some time has passed and you've had a chance to rework them. A time may come when you can actually use the letter as a basis for a conversation or another letter that you will send, but that time can come only further into the process.

These letters you are about to write should not be to people who have seriously abused or betrayed you. These letters should be to people with whom you have a painful but not completely fractured relationship. Often, immediate family members fit into this category. You tend to have unresolved issues with and unexpressed anger toward those you love the most. You may have longed to say things but were unable to do so. The guidelines listed below are intended simply to spark your own thoughts. You may or may not want to follow them exactly.

GUIDELINES FOR WRITING LETTERS

Begin by expressing gratitude and affection. If you are emotionally able to express gratitude and affection, it can provide a good foundation for your letter.

Clearly state the major unresolved issues. As clearly as you can, state what you think are the key problems in your relationship.

Express anger. Anger that is unexpressed can eat away at you. The safest way to deal with it is on paper. When you express your anger on paper, it is just for your eyes—expressing your anger on paper hurts no one, but it can relieve you of the powerful internal pressures repressed anger creates as it builds up inside you. This first draft of the letter is just for you. Expressing your anger can help you name and recognize the feelings you have been harboring. Your journal is a safe place for your anger. Expressing your anger immediately, without thinking about others, can often lead to more anger, or even to an addiction to anger, rather than to resolution. Expressing and processing the anger first on paper makes it easier for you to deal with another person in a healing way in real life and can help prevent the unwanted spontaneous eruptions unprocessed anger can cause.

Offer to forgive. If you are at a place in your life where you are truly able to forgive, offer your forgiveness. If you forgave long ago and put the hurt behind you, say so.

Ask for forgiveness. If you have become aware that you need to ask for forgiveness, by all means do so.

Suggest a resolution. If the person is still living, suggest a way to resolve your difficulties.

Offer a vision of what might be. If the person is still living and the relationship is ongoing, offer a picture of what you believe the relationship could become.

Suggest a plan. Suggest concrete steps for helping each other explore the possibilities you've just imagined.

To help stimulate your letter writing, some sentence stems are provided. But feel free to scratch through them and write on your own themes. Some of the sentence stems will not apply, of course, if you're writing to someone who is deceased.

If, in the course of writing, you feel emotionally overwhelmed and do not wish to continue, trust your instincts. It may be best to stop and take it up again at another time. It may be appropriate to consult a minister or therapist if your emotions continue to overwhelm you.

By all means, stop and pray as you write. You are writing to God and before God, whose help you can always call upon in prayer. You'll only have room to write one letter. In order to write more than one letter, copy these sentence stems onto another sheet of paper.

A LETTER . . .
to someone close, with whom you have unresolved issues

Dear _____

I am writing because I want to remove any barriers between us. I want to have a closer relationship with you. I care for you because

_____

_____

_____

I want to thank you for

_____

_____

_____

I have some painful issues I want to tell you about. They are:

_____

_____

Even though I care for you and value (or valued) our relationship, I am angry because

_____

_____

I feel

_____

_____

I have forgiven you in the past and am willing to forgive you now for

_____

_____

As I write this letter, I see that I need to ask your forgiveness for

_____

_____

I have some suggestions for how we can resolve the issues between us. They are:

_____

_____

_____

I dream of what our relationship can be in the future. My dream is

_____

_____

_____

Some concrete steps we can take to move into this dream are:

_____

_____

_____

Love,

_____

You may feel worse after getting the issues out in the open and expressing your feelings. Soon though, you will likely not only feel better, but you'll also function better. Unexpressed emotions and thoughts that were weighing you down have now been expressed, and you can now move on to living in God's present moment.

FOR THOSE WHO HAVE BEEN SEVERELY ABUSED

If you have been physically or sexually abused, it's important to work on healing slowly and with caring help.

If in the past you have worked through the basic story of your abuse with close friends, a member of the clergy, or a therapist, you are already moving closer to healing.

If you have never told your story of abuse to someone who could help you, it is important that you contact someone qualified to help you with these specific issues. Letter writing may be part of the work you do with this person, but it should be done under the supervision of a trained professional.

If you do write a letter, don't mail it until you have revised it and discussed it at length with someone qualified to help you.

A GUIDED MEDITATION: YOU BRING HEALING TO HURT RELATIONSHIPS

Get comfortable and ready to imagine . . .

Eternal love surrounds you. When you breathe in, you breathe in God's love; when you breathe out, you breathe out tension and pain. Notice your breathing in and your breathing out. Do not change it, just notice it.

Write out some of the painful feelings and stressful thoughts that came to you as you wrote your letters.

_____

_____

_____

Now that you have written them out, pray: "Lord, I give this to you. I hand over all of these feelings and thoughts to your everlasting mercy."

Jesus approaches you now. He places his hands on your shoulders and speaks comforting words to you. This is what he says:

_____

_____

_____

_____

_____

_____

_____

_____

_____

_____

_____

_____

_____

_____

_____

WHEN TO WRITE LETTERS YOU WILL SEND

The letters you are writing can help you clarify your thoughts and feelings and help you see the real issues. Your letter writing can help you move toward eventually having a face-to-face discussion with a person you care about. However, many people find that actually sending a letter to the person they care about, or reading a letter to them in person, is more effective and safer than having a discussion with that person. In a letter you get to say everything without being interrupted and before the conversation veers off track. Also, when a painful issue is broached in a letter, not having the sender present lessens the reader's feelings of guilt and creates a safer environment for him or her to respond.

Letters that primarily express gratitude can usually be sent once they are written. Letters that involve a degree of confrontation on problem issues should be revised before they are sent. Wait at least a week before working on a revision. It's usually best to get feedback on your first draft from someone you trust. The first draft was just for you; the revised version is for the person you care about.

Send the letter only after any storm of emotions has subsided and you can truly measure whether the letter will have a healing impact.

Sometimes it's best not to send the letter at all. The first draft of the letter was written primarily for you, not the other person. Writing the letter has enabled you to clarify your affection, conflict, and tension. You have been changed, and often this is enough.

If you do decide to rewrite and send the revised letter, do so after time, prayer, and, if possible, consultation with others.

A good book to help you with such letters is *Letters Home* by Terry Vance. It provides many actual letters and can help a great deal with the letter-writing process.

MEDITATION FOR CLOSING

Meditate on 1 Corinthians 13:1–7:

> *If I speak in the tongues of mortals and of angels, but do not have love, I am a noisy gong or a clanging cymbal. And if I have prophetic powers, and understand all mysteries and all knowledge, and if I have all faith, so as to remove mountains, but do not have love, I am nothing. If I give away all my possessions, and if I hand over my body so that I may boast, but do not have love, I gain nothing.*
>
> *Love is patient; love is kind; love is not envious or boastful or arrogant or rude. It does not insist on its own way; it is not irritable or resentful; it does not rejoice in wrongdoing, but rejoices in the truth. It bears all things, believes all things, hopes all things, endures all things.*

Take a few moments to write your response to this passage.

9 *Transforming Your Sorrows*

In the last chapter, you had a chance to work on healing some of the relationships of your life. In this chapter, you will look at the sorrows that influence your life and then take them to the God who can transform all sorrow.

Hurt held tightly within you can keep you from living fully in the present. To heal the present, it's essential to let go of unhealthy ties to the past. The undertow of sadness you have not dealt with affects everything in your present. You look at life through lenses colored by past pain, which prevent you from seeing this present moment clearly.

Now you will have a chance to look at your sorrows and let God begin the process of turning them into joy. You will transform old wounds into strengths and joys in the present. You will have a chance to write some stories of times of hurt and then to allow God to transform those hurts into strengths for the present.

In this chapter, you will

- return in a guided meditation to St. Hildegard's convent

- write stories of your sorrows

- review those stories from a different point of view

- invite God to heal your past pain

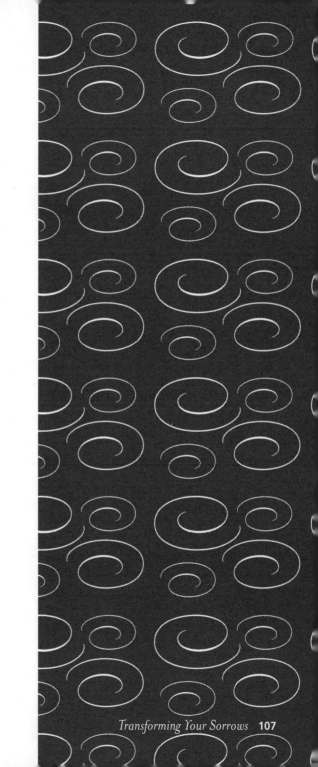

PRAYER OF ENTRANCE

Merciful and all-loving God,
when I open my soul before you,
you greet me with your comfort.
When I tell you of my sorrow,
you console me.
I am about to begin a time
of remembering past hurt and loss.
Walk with me.
Pain is no mystery for you,
for you have entered fully
into all this world's sorrows.
You hold my tears.
You remember my sighs.
Even when I thought myself abandoned,
you were there.
May my story be ever tied to yours.
Amen

A GUIDED MEDITATION: YOU RETURN TO THE CONVENT OF ST. HILDEGARD

Get comfortable and ready to imagine . . .

Now that you have let your prayer ease you and empty you of many current anxieties, it's time to take a trip back to another time. It's time to return to the convent of St. Hildegard of Bingen.

You stand in the ancient, shadowy hallway. A few small lamps flicker. Their moving shadows bring to mind not fear but mystery, a holy mystery that blends awe and comfort.

You hear the nuns chanting a hymn so beautiful that it could have come from heaven itself. It is a calming sound that brings you to a place of peacefulness.

What images and feelings come to you as you listen to the special music?

_____

_____

_____

_____

_____

_____

You hear steps now, the sound of sandals touching the stone floor. You know it is Jesus. You see that he is carrying a book and a lamp.

He walks up to you. His eyes shine with peacefulness. The light from the lamp illuminates his white robes.

His face speaks to you without words. His kind eyes communicate something directly to your heart.

What does Jesus' expression say to you?

_____

_____

_____

Jesus opens the door to the library and leads you in. You enter it and see many shelves filled with old books.

Jesus speaks to you: "I am the healer of hurt, the skilled physician who takes away pain. Hurt is lessened by the telling of stories."

Jesus hands you a white quill with which to write and holds the book open before you, the same book in which you are now writing. He asks, "Are you ready to face some of your stories?"

If you are not ready, come back to this chapter at another time.

If you are ready, write yes in the book, right here. _____

Jesus places the open book on the desk. He points to the many stacks of books in the library. He says, "Many of these books are about you. They contain pictures of the landmarks of your life, the joys, pains, sins, and accomplishments." He takes you to one shelf of books and pulls out a thick old volume. It is entitled *The Sorrows of My Life, as I Remember Them.*

Jesus continues: "In this book are pictures and stories of the sorrows of your life. These are the scenes of hurt as you hold them in your memory. As you thumb through this book, look at the pictures. They are pictures of you when you were hurt, key scenes from your past and the stories that go with the scenes."

You open the book and begin to look at the scenes and glance over the stories. Time slows almost to a standstill. You see much and yet only a short amount of time passes. Take your time and let the different pictures of the book fill your senses.

After you have finished browsing this book, Jesus takes you back to the desk. He asks you to sit, opens the book in which you are now writing, and asks you to write twelve short phrases that describe twelve landmark times of sorrow and hurt in your childhood and teenage years. If you can't come up with twelve phrases, write as many as you can.

TWELVE LANDMARK TIMES OF SORROW IN MY LIFE

1. _____

2. _____

3. _____

4. _____

5. _____

6. _____

7. _____

8. _____

9. _____

10. _____

11. _____

12. _____

Read your list carefully. Now pick two landmark times of sorrow that stand out. Later, if you choose, you can return to this list and work with some of the other landmark times, using a journal book or notebook. For now, write the stories of the two landmark times of sorrow you have chosen.

Write fast. Let the words flow. Just put your quill to the paper and tell the stories.

STORY 1

I passed through a landmark time of sorrow when _____

_____ , and this is the story of what happened.

_____

_____

_____

_____

_____

_____

_____

_____

_____

_____

_____

_____

_____

_____

_____

_____

_____

_____

_____

_____

STORY 2

I passed through a landmark time of sorrow when _____

_____ **, and this is the story of what happened.**

_____

_____

_____

_____

_____

_____

_____

_____

_____

_____

_____

_____

_____

_____

A HEALING MOMENT FOR EARLY SORROWS

Now that you have explored a landscape of pain, you look at Jesus. He sits in a chair and asks you to sit in a chair facing him. He takes your hands in his and passes the comfort of his heart to you through his hands.

Jesus now places the book in your lap. He speaks just the words you need and want to hear, words of healing and forgiveness. Write these words here.

_____

_____

_____

_____

_____

_____

_____

_____

_____

THE TRANSFIGURATION OF SORROW

The image of the resurrected Christ is an image of a Christ who still bears his wounds, though they are now transfigured. The wounds remain, but they radiate eternity. The wounds that were formed in the past and brought unendurable pain now bring immeasurable healing and light.

So it is with you. Healing can now come to you through your brokenness and painful sagas. From your shadows can now emerge a light that will brighten your world. Through Christ's wounds you are healed, and through your wounds you share that healing with others. You become strong in the broken places.

You have finished writing your stories of sorrow. Now it is time to explore sorrow's meaning. It is time for the wounds to be transfigured. Jesus shows you the stories of sorrow you just finished writing in your book. You review them.

Jesus tells you, "God the Father also knows your stories, but he sees them in a different light, from the point of view of eternity. He keeps each story in a book."

Jesus takes you to a very old book entitled, *God's Stories of Your Sorrows*.

"You see," says Jesus, "all of your stories are really twice-told tales, stories remembered from your point of view and stories remembered from God's point of view."

You open the book and look at the scenes of the two stories of sorrow that you recounted. This time, whatever the scene of sorrow, the holy light of God's presence surrounds it. In each scene of pain you see Jesus standing near you.

Take a moment to look at the two stories, the two scenes of pain, from God's vantage point. Review each scene, one at a time, noticing Jesus standing beside you. After you review each scene from God's point of view, work through the following writing meditations.

God's book of your memories is a special book; you can enter into it and step into God's light. All time—past, present, and future—is the same to the God who created time. The God who makes your present can heal your past. You can step into your past and invite God in.

STORY 1
My story from God's point of view

Review the first story of sorrow you wrote. Now write it again from God's point of view. See yourself in the scene with God's light surrounding you. Picture God's soft brightness surrounding your face and the faces of others.

_____

_____

_____

_____

_____

_____

_____

_____

_____

_____

_____

_____

_____

_____

_____

_____

_____

Describe how your face changes in the scene of pain now that God's light surrounds you.

_____

_____

_____

Now picture Jesus in the scene. What is the look on Jesus' face as he sees and hears your pain?

_____

_____

_____

What physical actions does Jesus take in this scene?

_____

_____

_____

Now you—the you of today—enter the scene. You speak to the you of that earlier time, the self who is experiencing the pain in this scene. You offer love and support. You offer to stand beside the frightened younger person you were then. What do you say?

_____

_____

_____

Now you introduce to Jesus the person you were in this scene. What do you say?

_____

_____

What does Jesus say to comfort and heal the person you were at this particular time in your life?

_____

_____

_____

Even the starkest losses and the most bitter tragedies hold within them ways in which you can be strengthened. They hold lessons for you. God is often working in you in an unseen way at such times. From God's point of view, redemption can be at work even in the midst of truly unexplainable hurt.

Jesus now tells the person you once were how redemption is at work in the midst of this particular story of sorrow. Write what he says.

_____

_____

_____

_____

_____

_____

_____

STORY 2
My story of sorrow from God's point of view

Review your second story of sorrow. Now write it again from God's point of view. See yourself in the scene with God's light surrounding you. Picture God's soft brightness surrounding your face and the faces of others.

Describe how your face changes in the scene of pain now that God's light surrounds you.

_____

_____

_____

Now picture Jesus in the scene. What is the look on Jesus' face as he sees and hears your pain?

_____

_____

_____

What physical actions does Jesus take in this scene?

_____

_____

_____

Now you—the you of today—enter the scene. You speak to the you of that earlier time, the self who is experiencing the pain in this scene. You offer love and support. You offer to stand beside the frightened younger person you were then. What do you say?

_____

_____

_____

Now you introduce to Jesus the person you were in this scene. What do you say?

_____

_____

_____

What does Jesus say to comfort and heal the person you were at this particular time in your life?

_____

_____

_____

Jesus now tells the person you once were how redemption is at work in the midst of this particular story of sorrow. Write what he says.

_____

_____

_____

_____

_____

_____

_____

_____

Take some time and write a prayer asking God to help heal your past pain.

_____

_____

_____

_____

_____

_____

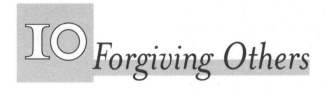

10 *Forgiving Others*

In the last chapter, you had a chance to take your sorrows to a loving God so that he could transform them. You looked at your past and worked on healing and enhancing your present. Now is the time to move forward and direct healing and forgiveness beyond you.

You won't find healing merely by taking a journey of purely inner exploration. Your self-exploration takes on value only when you let that exploration help you better love God's world and God's people. Genuine inner change always strengthens your connections with God's creation. True inner healing will lead to true outward healing. So pause now in your interior journey and take an outward look.

Not only have others hurt you, but you have also hurt others. Others have failed you, and you have failed others. You have used some of God's gifts well, but you have let other gifts atrophy. You don't need to strain to look for these failings; just let them emerge on their own.

The process you are engaged in can change your heart and make your inmost self supple again and responsive to God. Letting your regrets ripen into genuine sorrow, taking that sorrow to God, and seeking God's forgiveness are all central to your healing and transformation.

In this chapter, you will

- begin to turn your heart outward

- face the reality that not only have others hurt you, but you have also hurt others

- explore ways to forgive others

- explore ways to seek forgiveness

- meet the person with whom you are in conflict in a guided meditation

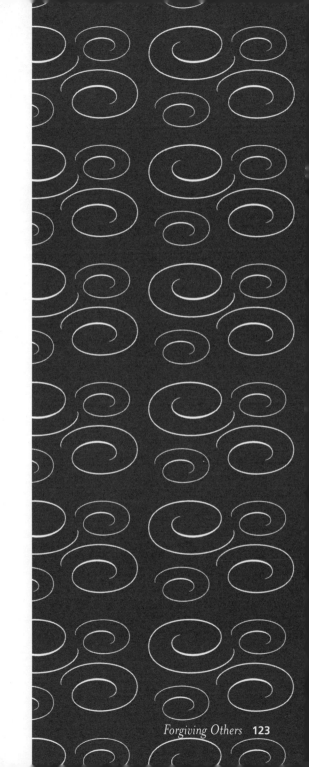

PRAYER OF ENTRANCE

Dear God,
you send your son Jesus
as one who called for repentance,
the remaking of the heart.
This is not your wish for me;
it is your command to me.
Help me regret when I need to regret and
seek forgiveness when I need to seek forgiveness.
At times I have loved well
and have been loved well.
At times I have stumbled,
and others have stumbled.
I come to you that you may
teach me to love when loving is hard.
I come to you that you may
guide me in the difficult art of loving.
I give my heart, my mind,
and my writing to you.
Turn all of this session
into a session of prayer,
a session of healing.
Amen

Although it is not a popular idea, taking responsibility for the failures in your life is central to healing. Consciously deciding to forgive and reaching out to those who have hurt you is vital to the transformation of your life. How can the strengths of your past help you love others better today? What regrets have emerged in your exploration of your life so far?

CONSCIOUSLY DECIDING TO HEAL THE HURTS OF RELATIONSHIPS

Working on your relationships is essential for repentance and a true change of heart. The following meditation is a blend of writing, prayer, and guided meditation.

In the guided meditation that follows, you will take the frustrations of your relationships to Jesus and will look to him for guidance. In the comfort that prayer brings, you may even want to write about some of the more severe breaches in your relationships, such as betrayal and desertion.

Some of these hurts happened a long time ago. Maybe the relationship you're focusing on was with a person who is no longer living. Or perhaps the person is an active part of your life now. Whether the hurt relationship is an old painful memory or a current stress, the blend of writing and meditation can help you in your personal healing. In the case of current relationships, it may even make it possible for you and the other person to reconcile and make a fresh start.

Though this long writing exercise allows only enough room to work with one relationship, it works best when you apply it to multiple relationships. To do this, you will need an additional notebook.

A note of caution: If you have suffered severe physical or sexual abuse and have never told your story to someone trained to help, please do so. Severe wounds can be too overwhelming to handle on your own, and other people are gifted and trained to help. If you have had that help in the past, this meditation can further your healing. If you have never had this help, you can seek it and use it in conjunction with what you are doing through this journal.

A GUIDED MEDITATION: YOU TAKE THE HURT TO JESUS

Get comfortable and ready to imagine . . .

Jesus takes a chair and sits in front of you. You can tell by the look on his face that he cares about you very much. He is surrounded by subdued light, and this light surrounds you too. Love and healing that cannot fully be expressed in words pass through the light, from Jesus to you. The light connects your heart with Jesus' heart.

Jesus speaks to you: "I am ready to hear all you have to say. There are no stories too awful for me to hear. There is nothing that you have done that I cannot forgive. I am here to listen to your story and dry your tears. I was with you at the times when you were hurt. I was walking right beside you.

"You can tell me now about a time when you were injured in a relationship. Tell that story here."

Jesus responds, and this is what he says:

Jesus continues: "I know that, having been hurt so deeply, you still carry some of the pain. I want you to pour out those feelings now. There is no need to hold back, for I am the one who is ready to absorb all the pain.

"What are you feeling right now?"

_____

_____

_____

_____

_____

_____

_____

_____

Jesus comforts you with these words:

_____

_____

_____

_____

_____

_____

_____

_____

Now Jesus says, "I know you have been injured, but I'm going to ask you to do a hard thing. I'd like you to step inside the heart of the other person. How would this situation look from that viewpoint? Think back to the story you just told me and tell it to me again, this time from that other person's point of view.

"Tell that story here."

Jesus asks, "Now that you've told this story from another viewpoint, what do you see or understand that you didn't see or understand before?"

Write your response.

_____

_____

_____

Jesus says, "Does it seem more possible now to forgive the other person?"

Write your response.

_____

_____

_____

Jesus says, "Do you think you are ready to forgive? Say yes only if you're ready. It is best to wait until the work of healing has brought you to the point of truly being able to forgive. Now are you ready to forgive?" _____

Jesus says, "Are you ready to meet this person in your prayer, your mind, and your imagination? You can practice love and forgiveness in your imagination. Sacred practice can generate compassion and understanding. This imagined forgiveness can help you to actually forgive in the real world. Are you ready to meet this person in this prayer session?" _____

If your answer is no, move on to another section of the journal and come back to this when you are ready. If your answer is yes, continue with the exercise.

_____, the person with whom you are in conflict, enters the room. He or she takes a seat facing you. Jesus stands to the side, putting a hand on your shoulder and a hand on the other person's shoulder.

What feelings, images, sensations, and memories cross your mind as you sit there with Jesus and the other person?

_____

_____

_____

_____

_____

_____

_____

_____

_____

_____

_____

_____

_____

_____

_____ speaks: "I'm ready now to hear what you have needed to tell me. I won't judge or react. I'm truly ready to listen."

Now say the things that have been too difficult to say up until now.

_____

_____

_____

_____

_____

_____

_____

_____

_____

_____

_____

_____

_____

_____

_____

Because of Jesus' presence, _____ is able to let go of fear and respond to you in a kind manner. He or she responds to what you have just said:

_____

_____

_____

_____

_____

_____

_____

You respond to what _____ has just said:

_____

_____

_____

_____

_____

_____

_____

_____

_____ asks you, "Are there ways I could have loved you better?" This time you really know that he or she wants to listen to you. You make a point to be kind as you explain how _____ could have loved you better.

_____ asks, "Will you forgive me?"

If you are truly ready to forgive this person, speak words of forgiveness that come from your heart:

_____

_____

_____

_____

_____

_____

_____

_____

Jesus now speaks to you: "You have spoken to _____ of your pain and have explained how he or she could have loved you better. Are you ready to hear how you may have failed in this relationship?"

If you are not ready, come back to this meditation at another time. If you are ready, continue with the meditation.

You look at _____, who sits across from you, and ask, "Are there ways I could have loved you better?"

_____ is kind as he or she explains how you could have loved him or her better.

_____

_____

_____

_____

_____

_____

_____

_____

_____

_____

_____

_____

_____

_____

_____

_____

_____

_____

_____

_____

Now that you have heard the ways you could have loved better, respond to
_____ with words from your heart.

_____

_____

_____

_____

_____

_____

_____

You ask, "Will you forgive me?"

_____ responds with words of forgiveness:

_____

_____

_____

_____

_____

_____

_____

PUT HEALING IN PICTURE FORM

Use this page to sketch a picture that symbolizes the mending of this relationship.

MEDITATION FOR CLOSING

Meditate on Psalm 51:6–10, 17:

> *You desire truth in the inward being;*
>   *therefore teach me wisdom in my secret heart.*
> *Purge me with hyssop, and I shall be clean;*
>   *wash me, and I shall be whiter than snow.*
> *Let me hear joy and gladness;*
>   *let the bones that you have crushed rejoice.*
> *Hide your face from my sins,*
>   *and blot out all my iniquities.*
>
> *Create in me a clean heart, O God,*
>   *and put a new and right spirit within me. . . .*
> *The sacrifice acceptable to God is a broken spirit;*
>   *a broken and contrite heart, O God, you will not despise.*

Take a few moments to write your response to this passage.

_____

_____

_____

_____

_____

_____

_____

II Finishing the Journey

You find yourself back in the convent of St. Hildegard of Bingen. You're in the main hallway, holding this journal. It's that deep dark hour just before the first hints of morning light filter in through the windows. You hear the soft ecstatic singing of the sisters drifting up the hall from the chapel. You hear steps moving toward you. Jesus is approaching. Beside him walks a nun in full habit. Both Jesus and the nun carry oil lamps, and the lights flicker in the hallway.

You look at Jesus and see that his eyes are shining brightly, the way a person's eyes dance when he or she is in the company of a close friend. You now see that the nun beside Jesus is Hildegard.

Jesus speaks to you: "I want to tell you more about your mentor, Sister Hildegard. She lives passionately, and she will teach you much in the next four days. She's a medical doctor, a composer, a poet, and an illustrator of manuscripts. She travels throughout Europe, preaching in major cathedrals. She boldly speaks the truth to bishops, priests, and nobility. A creative woman of imagination, she sees many visions."

You look at Hildegard and see an almost impish smile forming on her face. "Oh, he does go on like that sometimes," she says, feisty and self-assured.

Jesus smiles at her words.

You feel at ease around her.

You ask her, "What started you on such a career?"

"When I was forty-seven years and seven months old, the heavens were opened and a blinding light of exceptional brilliance flowed through my entire brain. It kindled my whole heart and breast like a flame, not burning but warming. It was after this that strength, human and divine, poured into me."

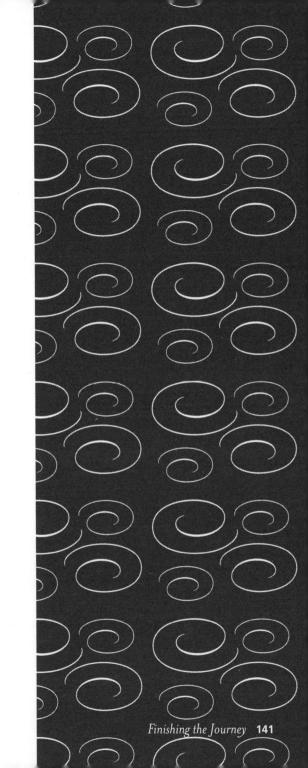

You believe what Hildegard says about herself. At the same time, you doubt that anything so amazing could happen to you.

Hildegard seems to read your mind. Her expression softens, and she says, "Everyone has visions. A gracious God interrupts the lives of all of God's children. Dramatic interruptions, vivid visions, happen far more commonly than you think. Less vivid moments of insight and sacred encounter are, in their own way, like visions too, and they happen all the time. You just have to take the time to notice them. They can saturate your living with God's nearness.

"You may not fully realize it yet, but your traveling through this journal, your writing, has been a sacred interruption, a vision. You grounded yourself in the present and let God comfort your fears. You lifted up your past to a compassionate God for healing. You looked at your present with a fresh perspective. You dreamed, you explored, and you searched your soul. Your stay at the convent this time will give you the opportunity to look back on your journey through this journal and sum up all you have learned.

"Visions help you grasp reality on a level both richer and deeper than abstract words. Visions reach to the core of the soul. During your stay you can seek visions that will fix the insights of your journaling firmly on your soul.

"Earlier I took you on a pilgrimage and gave you time to let insight and vision incubate in your soul. This time I will take you on another pilgrimage of sorts, a pilgrimage of waiting and prayer. You will have the chance to spend three days in the convent chapel, praying and sleeping through the night on the floor, just as many other seekers have done.

"I ask that you take part in a partial fast as you pray these three days. You will have just one meal a day, a delicious breakfast each daybreak.

"As you did on your earlier pilgrimage, you will have companions to pray with you throughout these three days. You will pick three of these companions, and I will be your fourth.

"Your first companion will be someone who can speak persuasively of God's comfort. This can be someone you know personally, such as a friend or a family member. Or you can choose someone you have never met, whose writings or words have touched you."

Who do you pick as companion number 1? _____

I picked _____ **as the companion to help me understand the God of comfort because**

_____

_____

_____

As soon as you pick your companion, this person emerges from the hall and joins you and Hildegard.

Hildegard continues, "Your second companion will be someone who can help you understand your past."

Who do you pick as companion number 2? _____

I picked _____ **as the companion to help me understand my past because**

_____

_____

_____

As soon as you pick your companion, this person emerges from the hall and joins you and Hildegard.

Hildegard says, "Your third companion will be someone who can help you understand your present."

Who do you pick as companion number 3? _____

I picked _____ **as the companion to help me understand my present because**

_____

_____

_____

As soon as you pick your companion, this person emerges from the hall and joins you and Hildegard.

After reminding you to carry your journal with you, Hildegard leads you and your three companions down the long shadowy hallway. The only light is from the lamp she carries.

The mystical light of oil lamps illuminates the chapel. The nuns gathered in choir sing soft plainsong. You imagine that these are the melodies of angels.

Suddenly a loud crash breaks the morning quiet: thunder. Rain and hail pound loudly on the chapel roof. Thunder booms every few moments. Then the clouds disperse, the storm ceases, and brilliant morning light streams through the stained-glass windows.

The storm and the calm that follows remind you of meeting the God of comfort in the beginning of your journal. You think back on what you learned about God's willingness to console you. You can work from memory or you can thumb back through your journal and look at what you wrote in chapter 2. It's been a while since you wrote in that section, and the insights that emerged at that time have had a chance to develop more fully. You now write some more.

WHAT I HAVE LEARNED . . .
about how God comforts me

_____

_____

_____

_____

_____

_____

_____

After you finish writing, you continue to pray quietly throughout the day. As the shadows of evening come, you begin to feel sleepy; after all, you've been up since before daylight. This is the Middle Ages, and people feel free to pull out their bedrolls and sleep on church floors. You notice other pilgrims preparing for bed. Companion 1, _____, passes you a bedroll. You spread it out on the floor, lie down, and quickly fall into a heavy sleep. Soon you dream, and in the midst of your dream you have a vision that sums up all you have learned in your journaling about meeting the God of comfort.

Write that vision here.

_____

_____

_____

_____

_____

_____

_____

_____

_____

You wake up as the first hints of daylight are shining in through the windows, and _____ (companion 1) reminds you that it's time for breakfast. It's none too soon; you haven't eaten for more than twenty-four hours.

Your companion leads you into the refectory and seats you at a small private table. Sister Hildegard brings you a heaping bowl of porridge.

Your companion asks you to recount any thoughts or visions you had during the day and night you spent in the church. Happily, you relate your thoughts along with the vision you had about meeting the God of comfort.

_____ listens attentively and says, "I have a couple of important insights to add to what you have told me that will help you meet God's comfort more readily in the future."

Write out what your companion says.

_____

_____

_____

_____

_____

_____

_____

_____

_____

You return now to the chapel. As dawn breaks, light pours in through the many stained-glass windows. They depict scenes from biblical history, such as Moses holding up his staff as the Red Sea parts, Jesus healing the blind man, and Jesus rising from the tomb. The windows remind you of the many ways God intervened not just in biblical history but in your personal history as well. You think back to the healing that came from the explorations of your past that you made in this journal. Since you first wrote about your past, your insights have had time to deepen and grow. You might want to review the passages in this journal on your past. Now you turn the page and write some more.

SOME WAYS . . .
my past is being healed in this process of journaling

_____

_____

_____

_____

_____

_____

_____

_____

After you finish writing, you pray throughout the rest of the day and bed down at nightfall. You fall into a profound sleep and in the middle of the night have a dream vision that sums up how your past is being healed.

Write that vision here.

_____

_____

_____

_____

_____

_____

_____

You wake up and then have breakfast with companion 2, _____. You recount your thoughts of the previous day and your vision from last night. Then your companion says, "I can see into people's hearts, and here are some additional ways your past is being healed, ways you might not have considered:

You return to the chapel after breakfast. You are homesick after days away from your normal routine. Your thoughts turn to your daily work, your family, and your favorite pastimes. Some of your daily worries intrude too. You reflect on ways your present is being healed by God. Since you first wrote about your present, your insights have had time to deepen and grow. You might want to review the passages you wrote in this journal that concern your present. Now you turn the page and write some more.

SOME WAYS . . .
my present is being healed in this process of journaling

_____

_____

_____

_____

_____

_____

_____

_____

After you finish writing, you pray throughout the rest of the day and then go to sleep at nightfall. You fall into a deep sleep and in the middle of the night have a dream vision that sums up the ways your present is being healed.

Write that vision here.

_____

_____

_____

_____

_____

_____

_____

You wake up and then have breakfast with companion 3, _____. You recount your thoughts of the previous day and your vision from last night. Then _____ says, "I can see into people's hearts, and here are some additional ways your present is being healed, ways you might not have considered:

_____

_____

_____

_____

_____

_____

_____

When your companion finishes, Hildegard steps up, taps you on the shoulder, and says, "You discover the tapestry of your soul not only through prayerful reflection but also through active creating. Your last day of retreat will be spent in one of the main work rooms."

She leads you down the hall, through a huge door, and into a large room crowded with desks. Many of the nuns are busy illustrating manuscripts. You pass desk after desk, stopping to admire these colorful drawings. One woman in the corner is writing a book of poems and visions. Another is composing some new hymns.

Hildegard says, "Now that you have summed up the different sections of this journal, the time has arrived for you to draw together all the insights from your journal to form an overall picture.

"One way to do this is to use your creativity. God speaks to us through poems, speeches, music, pictures—all sorts of art. As we write, paint, and make music,

God becomes more vivid to us; we brightly proclaim God's beauty and the beauty of God's creation.

"The poetry, the music, the art, the words all abide within you, waiting to be guided by God's Spirit. They yearn to be expressed outwardly. You don't have to be a great poet, a great artist, or a great writer—just express yourself with whatever talent you have been given and you will find yourself changed. The world is hungry for the truly beautiful, and you have within you much beauty to share. The more you express the beauty, the more the beauty flows through you and transfigures you.

"Let's start with poetry. Poetry doesn't have to rhyme. Poetry doesn't have to follow any set rules. Poetry is simply painting pictures with words, giving color, sound, and feeling to that which is otherwise inexpressible.

"One day I sensed God's Spirit. I looked out over a field that was haunted by God's beauty. God murmured to me, and I took out a quill and parchment. The following word pictures passed from my heart to my hand:

> *I am the breeze that nurtures all green things, encourages blossoms to flourish with ripening fruits. I am the rain coming from the dew that causes the grasses to laugh with the joy of life.*

"As I wrote these words, my experience of the field that day was sealed and completed, just as a sealing and a completion took place in my soul.

"When you write poetry, you paint pictures with words."

Quickly write down some phrases—word pictures—that express the healing that has taken place in you during your journaling through this book. The words don't need to rhyme, and they can come in any order. The words are inside you, just waiting to be written. They will begin pouring out as soon as you touch your pen or pencil to this paper.

A POEM . . .
that sums up the insights of my journaling

_____

_____

_____

_____

_____

_____

_____

_____

_____

_____

_____

_____

_____

_____

After you finish your poem, Hildegard continues, "We express the ineffable, seal and complete it, and give it voice in drawings, sculptures, paintings, and images that we craft. You do not need to be a great artist to craft truly healing, liberating images. The foggiest sketch can take on great meaning for you. The other sisters and I often spend long hours painting the visions of our imaginations to illuminate manuscripts.

"In just a moment, you will draw an image from your soul, maybe an image you did not even know abided there. When you touch your pen or pencil to paper, it will start to emerge. For now just use your pen or pencil; later, if you are so inclined, you can paint or sculpt the image.

"Throughout your writing, God has whispered a message to you. There is an image within you that can be a symbol of what God has been whispering to you.

"This symbol is already in you, anxious to come out. Just touch your pen or pencil to paper, start making a line, and then the picture will unfold before you."

Quickly begin to sketch a picture that will become a symbol to you of what God has been speaking to you throughout your writing journey.

A PICTURE . . .

of what God has been whispering in my heart throughout this writing journey

Look at your picture. What message does God seem to be whispering to your soul?

_____

_____

_____

God is always calling you to change, to reform your heart so that you can become more loving, more caring, more self-giving. What in your picture expresses God's call to you to change?

_____

_____

_____

How does your picture express God's healing in your heart?

_____

_____

_____

You have looked through the lenses of memory, vision, poetry, and art at your overall experience of journaling through this book. Now it's time to sum up everything before God.

Gather in the beauty and healing that have been growing within your heart and write a prayer of thanks to God for guiding your writing.

A PRAYER . . .

of thanks that sums up my journey of healing throughout this book

Bibliography

Adams, Kathleen. *Journal to the Self: 22 Paths to Personal Growth*. New York: Warner Books, 1990.

Adams, Kathleen. *The Way of the Journal: A Journal Therapy Workbook for Healing*. Lutherville, Md.: Sidran Press, 1993.

Biffle, Christopher. *The Castle of the Pearl*. New York: Barnes and Noble, 1983.

Bonaventure. *The Tree of Life*. In *Bonaventure,* translated by Ewert Cousins. The Classics of Western Spirituality series. New York: Paulist Press, 1978.

Peace, Richard. *Spiritual Journaling: Recording Your Journey toward God*. Colorado Springs, Colo.: NavPress, 1998.

Pennebaker, James. *Opening Up: The Healing Power of Expressing Emotions*. New York: Guilford Press, 1997.

Rainer, Tristine. *The New Diary: How to Use a Journal for Self-Guidance and Expanded Creativity*. Los Angeles: J. P. Tarcher, 1978.

Vance, Terry. *Letters Home: How Writing Can Change Your Life*. New York: Pantheon Books, 1998.

Wills, Garry. *Augustine*. New York: Viking Press, 1999.

Contact the Authors

Deacon Eddie Ensley and Deacon Robert Herrmann are nationally known speakers. They are available for parish missions, conferences, retreats, days of renewal, leaders' days, catechist training workshops, lay ministry formation, clergy days, and journaling workshops. For more information, contact them at 1-800-745-4416 or e-mail them at **yahula@worldnet.att.net**. You can also visit them online, at **http://www.contemplative.catholic.org**, or write to them at Contemplative Brothers, Box 8065, Columbus, Georgia 31808.

Deacon Eddie Ensley is an international speaker and Catholic retreat leader who describes himself as a "miner in search of the forgotten riches of the spiritual past." The author of numerous articles and books, including *Visions: The Soul's Path to the Sacred* (Loyola Press, 2000), he holds a graduate degree in theology and is known for making spiritual practices accessible to the average person.

Deacon Robert Herrmann has more than twenty years of experience in leading retreats. An athlete and former track coach, he is widely respected for his spiritual journaling expertise and his teachings on contemplative prayer. He holds a certificate in pastoral ministry from Loyola University New Orleans.

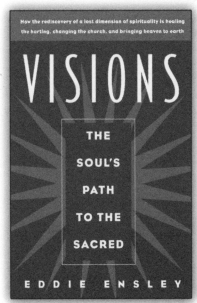